The Art and Craft of
Handmade Cards

THE ART AND CRAFT OF

Handmade Cards

DIANE MAURER-MATHISON

WATSON-GUPTILL PUBLICATIONS / NEW YORK

First published in 2003 by Watson-Guptill Publications,
a division of VNU Business Media, Inc.,
770 Broadway, New York, New York 10003
www.watsonguptill.com

Library of Congress Control Number: 2003104065

ISBN 0-8230-2183-1

Printed in China

First printing, 2003

1 2 3 4 5 6 7 8 9 / 11 10 09 08 07 06 05 04 03

NOTES ON THE ART
Refer to the pages cited below for information about the handmade cards
shown and the techniques that were used to create them.
On the front cover (clockwise from upper left): Mary Howe (page 110), Lea Everse
   (page 97), Joan B. Machinchick (page 108), and Claudia K. Lee (page 60).
On the back cover (clockwise from top right): Vonda Jones (page 139), Diane
   Maurer-Mathison (page 7), Susan Joy Share and Roni Gross (page 9),
   and Jill Quillian (page 133).
Page 2: Diane Maurer-Mathison (page 92).
Page 5: Lea Everse (page 74) and Fred B. Mullett (page 44).
All art not credited to a specific artist was produced by the author.
All line art by Jeffery Mathison.

Acquisitions Editor: Joy Aquilino
Editor: Meryl Greenblatt
Designer: Barbara Balch
Production Manager: Hector Campbell
Principal Typeface: Mrs. Eaves

For Lea Everse and Fred Mullett,

whose design sense, innovative ideas, and willingness to share
technique make showing their work such a pleasure.

ACKNOWLEDGMENTS

Many thanks to all the artists whose inspiring card designs and
calligraphy fill this book.

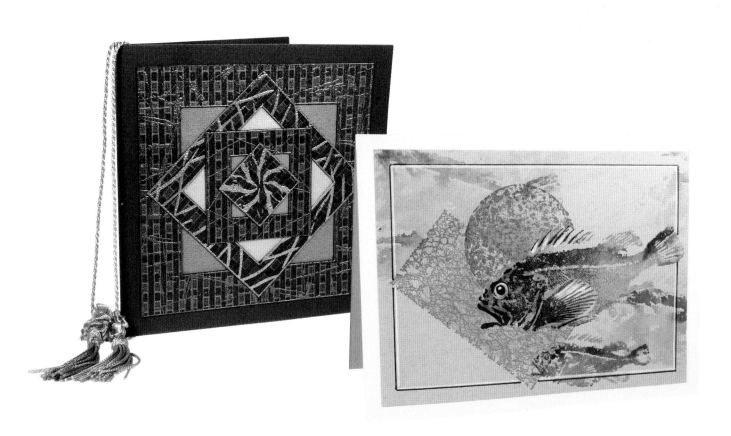

Contents

This three-panel card with a heart-shaped opening reveals a textured pattern made by applying crumpled plastic wrap to a paper washed with diluted inks. (See page 34 for technique.)

Preface

Whether sent through the mail or delivered in person, the handmade card brings with it a message that goes beyond the words written inside. It says, "I cared enough about you to steal time away from my busy schedule and create something special for you."

Picking out a cyber-card and e-mailing it to a friend to say, "Happy Birthday" or "I thought about you today" just doesn't have the same effect. It may be good to hear from a friend or even charming to see Felix the Cat racing across your computer screen to music for the moment, but a few minutes later the delight fades and you are left feeling a little empty. There's no card from a faraway friend or relative to proudly display on the sideboard during the birthday party or to lovingly stand in your studio or living room to remind you throughout the week that an old friend or schoolmate still thinks about you.

A diamond pattern "quilt" card by Martha Sparks. Quilt stamp by Stamp Francisco, Pansy paper by Design Originals.

ALASKA VOCABULARY
QUIZ

1. Baidarka

2. *The Bush*

3. **Mukluk**

4. *Muktuk*

5. Sourdough

PASSENGER   PASSE

ANCHORAGE

PETERSBURGH

BROOKLYN

ARLINGTON

PASSENGER

A pop-up wedding announcement by Susan Joy Share and Roni Gross.

What a thrill it is to sort through the piles of catalogs, bills, and junk mail that fill our mailboxes today and spy a hand-written envelope. It's practically cause for celebration! If the envelope is embellished with stamping, stenciling, or another form of decoration, receipt of the card is even more wonderful. It's hard to decide whether to quickly open it first to see the prize inside or wait until the other mail is opened and carry it off to a special comfy chair to slowly peel back the envelope flap and savor its contents.

When several of my paper artist and calligrapher friends first embraced computer technol-ogy. I received quite a few e-mail notes and cards instead of the beautifully lettered postcards and greeting cards I'd come to love. When my wishing for the good old days went unheeded, I decided to arm-twist just a bit. Instead of sending my usual plain cards with hand marbled or paste-painted panels on the front, I added gold-embossed Celtic dec-oration and layered different col-ored papers to make even the "Hi, how are you" cards look sumptu-ous. Just a few minutes more time spent made a difference and we are back to exchanging wonderful cards that are revisited over and over as keepsakes or framed and placed on our walls.

If you are already an artist or experienced craftsperson, you're sure to find some new ideas and techniques in this book that will help you add to your repertoire of card and envelope designs. If you are a novice paper artist or a person who still laments that she or he is not creative, you're in for a sur-prise. You'll be amazed at how easy it is to master paper decorating and card-crafting techniques and create a handmade card or invitation that will delight the recipient and mark special events with a wonderful gift—an artful greeting.

preparing the CANVAS

Just as a painter must consider the canvas on which he or she will create a painting and rule out the use of cardboard or other inferior material that will deteriorate quickly, card artists must also make sure they're working with quality papers that won't fade in a few weeks, crack when folded, or absorb and feather the ink when the final lettering or greeting is added. It is also important to know some basic techniques for working with paper so that, for example, the background papers or canvas on which your card design is built are cut square, torn evenly, or layered with other compatible papers without the tell-tale shiny spots that whisper of excess glue applied. It's a good idea to practice card-making techniques before attempting them on expensive paper. None of the techniques are difficult, but you'll feel more confident if you practice them several times. As a result, you'll showcase your art to its greatest advantage.

Stars and Stripes, a variation on a paste paper accordion-fold card by Mary Howe.

Choosing and Purchasing Base Papers and Card Stock

The type of paper you choose to form the base of your card will depend upon the type of card you're making and whether you plan to collage several layers of materials on top of it, letter on it using liquid inks, or fold it in several places to create a pop-up greeting. For a card that's folded a number of times without expanding, like a tea bag card, you'll probably want to start with a thin handmade paper, but for most other types of cards, a good quality cover-weight paper or card stock is your best choice.

Card stock is readily available in every imaginable color in most art supply, scrapbooking, stamping, and stationery stores. It has a smooth surface that won't cause your pen to bump across or bleed into it if you choose to letter on it, is thick enough to support layers of paper and embellishments attached to it, and folds nicely without cracking. Card stock is often sold flat or prescored with matching envelopes.

Ready-made cards and matching envelopes can also be pur-chased in packs through art supply catalogs, stationery shops, and craft supply stores. These are often made from a high quality drawing paper, which will get you started making beautiful cards without the delay of measuring, cutting, and folding. It's always less expensive to "start from scratch," however, so I usually begin with the least expensive good quality base materials and save my money for exotic papers I can layer on top of them.

Right: A tea bag folded card by Sandy Stern featuring stamping, dry embossing, and stenciling. Stamp by My Sentiments Exactly.

Assembling Basic Card-making Equipment

Although cards can be made with a minimum of equipment on a small table in your kitchen or den, card-making can become addictive. When it does, you'll not only look for more room to spread out and store materials, but will also want to have some basic equipment at hand to help you cut and fold cards accurately. That way you can quickly move on to the more creative parts of card design.

Paper cutter. If you have access to a large paper cutter, preferably with a bar to hold paper in place so that you can cut several sheets at once, you can easily divide sheets of paper for your greeting cards. A large paper cutter allows you to purchase large sheets of paper (or get cast-offs from a local commercial printer) and cut

Below: Some of the materials and equipment used to make handmade cards and envelopes, including various types of paper punches, coloring agents, rubber stamps, embossing pads, envelope templates, skeleton leaves, and foils.

smaller card-sized pieces from them. It's the most economical way to work.

Craft knife and metal ruler. If you don't have a paper cutter, you can make accurate paper cuts by using an X-acto knife and yard-long metal straightedge or steel square to guide the blade. Stock up on blades and always use a sharp one to make clean cuts. Unintentional ragged edges always show, and will ruin your card.

Smaller squaring and ruling devices. Although a steel square and long metal ruler are indispensable for squaring and cutting large sheets of paper, a plastic triangle or small X-acto knife comes in handy when cutting, scoring, and folding smaller papers. One of my favorite tools is a plastic triangle with calibrations and grids for measuring and squaring made by the C-Thru Ruler Company. The grid on this versatile tool can be read on dark or light paper and the triangle has a metal edge for cutting, too!

C-Thru rulers are similarly outfitted with a grid and metal cutting edge. Buy the longest one you can find. Although many artists like to use rulers with a cork backing that prevents the ruler from slipping out of position, I prefer the C-Thru with its handy grid, which assures you that you're cutting "on the mark."

A centering ruler with "O" as the center mark is helpful in determining the center of a card for lettering, creating windowed openings, or accurately placing decorative elements.

Cutting mat. A self-healing cutting mat should be placed under the paper being cut. Don't try to use cardboard as a cutting surface—it rapidly dulls knife blades. A piece of glass with the edges taped (so it won't cut you) is an alternative cutting surface that some card artists claim gives them a smoother cut.

Scissors. An assortment of scissors with long blades and short decorative ones are used for card-crafting. They, too, should be sharp and clean without glue or adhesive on the blades from previous craft adventures.

Hole punches. Various types of paper punches and decorative hole punches with shapes like birds, shamrocks, and geometric designs are useful for creating a decorative border for your cards. A Japanese screw punch with different sized bits is also a great tool for card-making; when you apply pressure on the handle, the bit rotates, creating a hole in the paper. It's perfect for making small holes around the edges of a card through which you may want to weave narrow ribbon or raffia.

Awl or large weaving needle. An awl or weaving needle is helpful for scoring papers to be folded.

Bone folder. A bookbinder's bone folder is used for folding and creasing papers. It is also used to press out air bubbles and wrinkles when gluing papers and fabrics to each other.

Glue brushes. You may find that working with dry adhesives makes your card-making easier. On the other hand, if you are from the old school and prefer working with liquid adhesives, depending upon the size of your task at hand, purchase a few large and small glue brushes. A large brush is necessary when applying glue to a large area, but a small brush is much more convenient for coating a small strip of paper to add to a collage or laying down a narrow line of glue to press a ribbon into. I find slightly stiff, flat, synthetic bristle brushes from art supply stores fine for most jobs.

Damp sponge. Always keep a damp sponge nearby when working with liquid adhesives. It helps remove glue from your fingers before it gets transferred to your papers.

Other materials and equipment used for specific card projects will be noted in subsequent chapters.

Basic Techniques for Beginning a Card or Envelope

If you haven't had much experience working with paper before, some of these techniques may feel awkward at first. With a little practice, however, these steps to transforming a sheet of blank paper into a folded card on which you can create a sumptuous greeting or invitation will become second nature to you.

FINDING PAPER GRAIN

Most machine-made papers, like planks of wood and pieces of fabric, have what's known as a "grain," or direction in which the fibers align themselves. On the other hand, the fibers of handmade papers are distributed at random,

so they usually do not have a particular grain direction. When making cards with machine-made paper, it is important to note and keep track of the grain direction. Papers on which the fold line runs parallel to the grain of the paper will crease easily without cracking, and will hold their shape. Papers folded against the grain will crease unevenly, crack often, and be generally uncooperative.

To test for grain direction in a sheet of paper, bend the sheet in half. If the paper easily collapses in on itself, you're bending with the grain. If the paper resists your efforts, you're bending cross-grain. Test the paper in each direction and then pencil an arrow on it to mark the grain direction.

CUTTING PAPER AND CARD STOCK

There are several ways to divide paper. Making straight cuts is easiest with a good quality paper cutter. If you plan to create greeting cards as a business or even an ongoing hobby, it makes sense to invest in a good cutter with a bar to assist you in holding material in place while you lower the chopping arm. Care must be exercised in using

---

Below left: Determining paper grain. Paper folded with the grain will bend easily and fold without cracking.

Below right: Using an X-acto knife and metal-edged triangle to divide paper.

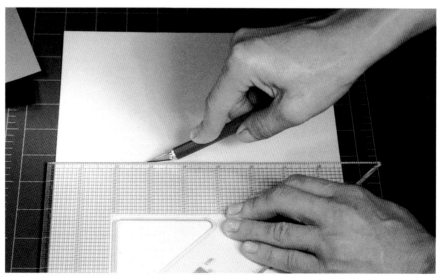

this type of cutter, however, as the blade remains very sharp.

If you don't have a paper cutter, you can use an X-acto knife and metal-edged ruler to slice through papers. Hold the knife upright and make sure you change blades often, so that cuts are clean, not ragged. Rotary paper trimmers can also be used to cut papers.

CREATING A CARD TO FIT A PURCHASED ENVELOPE

If you don't intend to make custom envelopes to fit your cards, you'll probably want to consider cutting your card stock to a size that fits into a standard envelope. Various envelope sizes, ranging from very tiny to very large, are readily available in bulk from printers, craft stores, office supply stores, and many department stores. Common sizes are A-2 (4⅜" x 5¾"), A-6 (4⅞" x 6½"), and A-7 (5¼" x 7¼"). If you plan to make long, narrow cards, # 10 business-sized envelopes (4⅛" x 9½") are easy to find.

In general, your card should be approximately ¼" smaller than its envelope. Keep in mind, however, that thick cards with lots of collaged panels or embellishments may require a bit more room.

For a simple folded card whose front and back panels are the same size, you can determine the width of the card and just double the size of one of the panels to determine the length of your unfolded card stock. For instance, to make a card to fit a purchased 5¼" x 7¼" envelope you would cut out a piece of card stock that measures 7" x 10" and fold it in half.

CREATING A CUSTOM-DESIGNED ENVELOPE

It is also easy to create your own envelope by steaming open a purchased one and using it to make a pattern you can trace around on plain or decorated, light to medium weight papers. You can enlarge or decrease its size by using a ruler to draw parallel lines around the perimeter of the first pattern. Another option is to trace around one of the many plastic envelope templates on the market, some of which allow you to create a card and envelope in one piece.

SCORING AND FOLDING

Scoring, using a bone folder, awl, weaving needle, or other tool to crease a paper's surface, prepares a paper for folding. Your fold lines will be sharper and neater if you slowly and carefully score paper or card stock first. Folding along the paper's grain is recommended.

To score for a card fold, measure and mark the fold line on the intended outside of the card with the tip of an awl and then hold a C-Thru triangle, metal triangle, or other squaring device against the desired fold line. Using the triangle to guide you, drag the point of the scoring tool down the length of the triangle. The object is to indent, but not break, the surface of the card stock to prepare it for folding. Then bend away from, not into, the fold line to crease it. Sharpen the crease by running the edge of the bone folder down the fold line. To avoid adding a shine to your folded card, you may want to cover it with a piece of tracing paper before sharpening the fold.

To score a sheet of card stock in preparation for folding, drag the point of your scoring tool down the length of a metal-edged ruler or triangle.

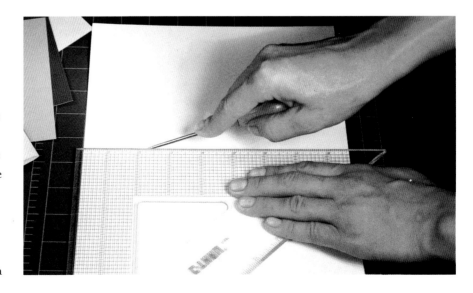

Exploring Basic Card Structures

There are many ways to fold paper or card stock to create a base for further decoration. Most greeting cards are made to stand and are usually folded once along the long edge for a vertical portrait format or positioned so that the fold is along the top edge for a landscape shape. Thin papers are often folded twice in the traditional "French fold" style to make them sturdy enough to stand on their own. A "gate fold" with a central panel flanked by two side panels, each measuring half the central panel's width, is another popular card design.

CREATING AN ACCORDION-FOLDED CARD

The "concertina" or accordion-folded card is perhaps the most versatile, as the number of accordion folds can be varied to create a simple trifold card or a long expanding card that stretches out several feet in length.

To cut accordion-folded pages, use a large paper cutter or an X-acto knife and a ruler to slice off a strip of paper. The grain of the paper should run vertical, parallel to the vertical fold lines, and the width of the paper strip should match the measurement you chose for the height of your card. Don't worry about the length of the paper. You can always cut several strips and join them later to make a longer card with folded pages.

Prepare to fold the pages by measuring off each page width for the entire length of the paper strip and making a faint mark with the tip of your awl or weaving needle. Place your squaring triangle at

Portrait and landscape format "mosaic" cards by Paula Beardell Krieg.

every other mark and score the paper by lightly running the awl or needle against the edge of the squaring device. Next, turn the paper over and score the remaining pages on the opposite side of the paper. Use your bone folder to crease the paper (away from the indentation) to create the first page of your card. Keep accordion-folding until you reach the end of your paper, making sure that the top and bottom edges of the paper always line up. To add length to your card, join similarly folded pages together as shown (facing page, top). Finish your page strip by cutting off any excess that is not wide enough to be used as a page.

Note: A renegade method of folding, which goes much faster, can be accomplished by measuring and scoring the first fold and then turning the paper over and using the first folded page as a guide to determine where to score and fold the next. If you keep turning your paper over, making sure the tops

and bottoms of your pages line up, always using the previous fold as a guide, you may find, as I do, this method works perfectly and that the page size remains constant without expanding throughout your folding.

An accordion-folded structure is a great beginning for a "flag

card" with a word or two written on slips of paper attached to an accordion-folded spine. You can also cut a gradually wider waved pattern along the top of the paper to form a card that expands in height as well as length as you open it.

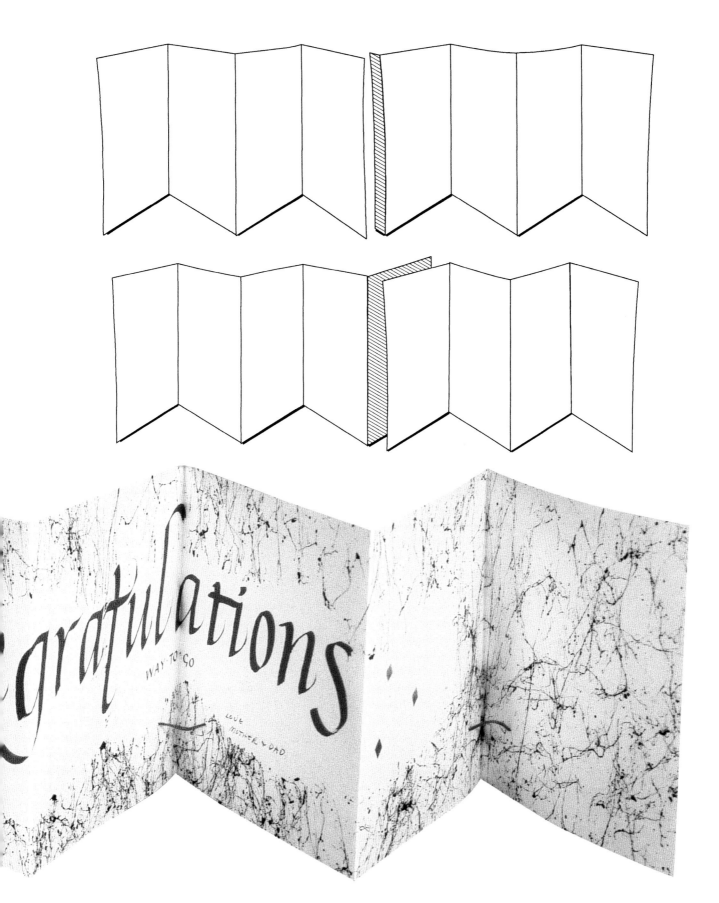

THE PAMPHLET-STITCHED CARD

By stitching three or more sheets of folded paper together, you can make a simple base for an elaborate card. The top sheet, or card cover, should be slightly wider and longer than the other pages. It can be made of card stock or other heavy paper. A second sheet may be thin Oriental or lace paper and the third sheet text-weight paper on which a personal message or invitation can be written. Fold each of the sheets in half with the grain running vertically, sandwich them together, and clamp or hold them in place while you make three stitching holes through the sheets simultaneously. Then, using embroidery floss, gold thread, or other stitching material 2½ times the height of your card, sew them together as shown (below right).

Below left: A pamphlet-stitched card joined with waxed linen thread by Sandy Hogan.

Below: Pamphlet stitching. Begin sewing through the center hole in the card pages, leaving an 8" or longer length of cord (or "tail") extending from it. Carry the cord through to the center of the card up to the top hole (A). Enter that hole and carry the cord over the cover of the card down to the bottom hole (C). Pull the cord taut as you continue. Bring the cord through to the center of the card again and then reenter the center hole (B) to bring the cord through to the cover of the card again. Position the two ends of the cord (the original tail and the new end you just brought through) so that they straddle the long length of cord running from hole A to hole C, and tie them together to finish. If you prefer, you can begin sewing on the inside of the folded pages and knot them together inside as well to finish the card.

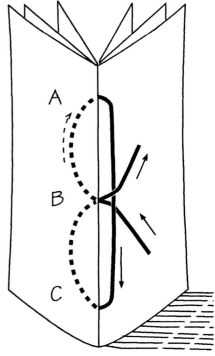

Creating a Deckle or Decorative Paper Edge

Although most of the time you'll probably work with a basic portrait or landscape card fold with straight edges, you may also want to experiment with card designs having a deckle or decorative paper edge. The edge can be created before the card is folded in half or after the fold is made. Either way, it is a good idea to practice on a scrap of paper identical to that of your card to see how the paper tears.

Free-form Tearing

For free-form tearing, remove approximately ½" of the paper along the bottom or edge of a card by tearing away from you to create a clean ragged edge, or toward you to create a more textured edge revealing the paper's core. Many card artists like to use colored pencils or pens to add color to this exposed paper edge.

Torn-paper edges are layered on this card by Lynell Harlow. Embossing paste pushed through a brass stencil and background coloring made with iridescent paint sticks are also featured.

Using an Art Deckle Ruler

Another way to create a decorative edge resembling the beautiful deckle edges that appear on hand-made papers is to use Design A Card's Art Deckle Ruler. To use this, simply lay your paper face down and, using an upward motion, remove a ½" strip by pulling it over the serrated teeth of the Art Deckle Ruler. On heavy cover-weight paper or very fibrous papers, you may want to lay down a line of water with a paintbrush (using the ruler's edge as a guide), let it seep in for a moment, and then pull the paper over the teeth of the Ruler.

Using Edging Scissors, Cutters, and Punches

Rolling trimmers and edging scissors in various patterns from pseudo-deckle edge to scallop and Victorian wave designs can be used to trim the front panel of a folded card. Buy these with the longest blades possible. If you must make several cuts to span the edge of the card, for best results cut partway and then stop and line up the teeth with the cut pattern before continuing. Rolling trimmers will cut a much longer strip of paper, but may not have the decorative pattern you desire.

Punches in the shape of hearts, geometric designs, or various animals can be used to create decorative holes across the bottom of a card. Some people like to save the shaped paper that is removed by the punch to glue inside the card and repeat a theme. Another tool that is even more useful is the corner punch. Available in several designs, it can give your card or background papers attached to it a finished and sophisticated look without appearing "cute." The piece removed by the punch can be used to accentuate a design by placing it near the central panel from which it was removed. The only problem is that sometimes these large punches are hard to operate. Resist the urge to hit

A magazine photocollage card with a cut decorative edge by Lea Everse, who accentuated her design by placing the corners removed by a Fiskars Regal Corner Edger near the central panel from which they were removed.

yours with a sledge hammer if it refuses to cut. Usually leaning over and pressing on it with both hands or stepping on it will help slice through heavy paper. Lea Everse, who often uses these to make magnificent cards, suggests periodically punching through sandpaper to keep them sharp.

Choosing and Layering Background Materials

Background papers—those papers layered beneath a stamped design, folded tea bag medallion, photo, or other focal point on your card—don't have to stand, fold well, or do anything special. Because of this they can be made of almost any material. There is an unbelievable variety of handmade and machine-made papers for card artists to choose from.

Beside the standard drawing, charcoal, and pastel papers, decorative papers include such types as Unryu, Thai Crinkle, Indian bark, Egyptian papyrus, Thai Reversibles (laminated so each paper is a different color on its reverse side), banana, lace, Indian silk, velour and velvet, hemp, and corrugated. There are papers with all kinds of embossed designs, and handmade specialty papers made from flower petals, grass, pine needles, denim, and dog fur. These are just a few examples!

Marbled, paste-painted, batik, and leaf-printed papers can be purchased (or made by you) and layered with other papers or adhered to folded card stock to create a beautiful base for further embellishment. They look great when used to frame a gift, charm, or cast-paper decoration attached to

the front of a card. Look for a wide range of papers in art and paper supply shops or in mail order art supply catalogs. (See the "Suppliers" section on page 141 for more information.) Fabric can also be adhered to your card base to showcase or set off other elements featured on your greeting cards.

WORKING WITH ADHESIVES

Deciding whether to use an archival glue, paste, glue stick, or adhesive film to bond papers and fabrics depends upon what kind of project you're working on and its intended lifespan. Double-sided tapes such as ATG Tape, spray adhesives, and adhesive films like Cello-Mount will make your work go faster. Avoid using rubber cement as it will bleed through papers and fabric in a few years. Ordinary cellophane tape will yellow and dry out in a few years, too. Unlike purchased cards, most handmade cards are treasured and often wind up in scrapbooks passed from one generation to another. I have several Victorian valentines that are in great shape because high quality materials were used.

I avoid using liquid glues for layering base papers in card-making

whenever possible to avoid the bleed-through or wrinkling that sometimes occurs when very thin papers or fabrics are adhered to each other.

A number of double-sided adhesive films on the market today can be used with more success. Some, like Cello-Mount, consist of a thin sheet of adhesive film sandwiched between two slippery protective papers. To use it, you peel away one protective sheet to expose the adhesive and apply your paper or fabric to it. When you peel away the other sheet, you're left with a sticky-backed piece of paper or cloth.

Other mounting adhesives, for example, those made by Stick-Ease or Neschen, consist of a roll of very thin adhesive coated onto a release paper. They're a bit more tricky to work with, but their adhesive properties are great.

One of the latest and easiest methods of applying glue to papers to bond them to each other is to use a Xyron machine. Using neither heat nor electricity, this amazing machine applies adhesive or lamination to your paper when you feed your paper into it with a hand crank. Many card artists such as Lea Everse, who's known for her extravagant multilayered cards, swear by it.

*U*nderstanding Color

When layering papers or choosing and arranging elements for your card designs, it is important to choose colors that complement each other. The most interesting design and technically excellent stamping, stenciling, collage arrangement, or other card-decorating technique will yield a disappointing greeting if the elements clash with each other or are so close to each other in intensity that they produce a boring card. The background paper alone can influence the colors of the papers layered on it and make everything look flat or visually exciting. In card design, where many elements are brought together in one piece, some knowledge of color mixing and interaction is critical to producing a successful work.

If you don't have experience mixing colors, spend a little time studying a color wheel to help you make more successful cards and invitations. By referring to a color wheel you can see how mixing the primary colors red, blue, and yellow can yield a range of other colors or hues. The three secondary colors, purple, orange, and green, are made by mixing two primaries together (for example, blue + yellow = green). The six tertiary colors are made by mixing a primary with an adjacent secondary color (for example, blue + green = blue-green). Your color palette can be further extended by tinting these colors with white or shading with black to change their value and make them darker or lighter. In a card design, dark colors appear to recede, while lighter ones advance.

Shades of the same colors harmonize beautifully in this card by Rona G. Chumbook.

Another factor to consider when choosing a color palette for your card is the temperature of your colors. Cool colors such as blue, green, and purple, which remind one of mountains or oceans, appear to recede in a composition while warm ones—red, orange, and yellow—leap forward. Although this may seem like information more important to painters than card designers, some knowledge of color theory can help you choose papers and colors that work with each other and lessen the time you spend placing papers over each other to see if you like the results. It can also prevent the color of a background paper from overpowering, for example, a delicate folded or quilled design placed on it. Understanding color theory can also prevent collage elements on your cards from becoming an irritating jumble of colors.

Four harmonious color schemes to experiment with when choosing papers for your cards or mixing colors for paper-decorating techniques to be used on your cards are the following:

Monochromatic. Using tints and shades of a hue, such as light, medium, and dark green, creates a monochromatic color scheme.

Analogous. Create this type of color scheme by using hues adjacent to each other on the color wheel, such as blue, blue-green, and green.

Complementary. These color compositions are formed by using

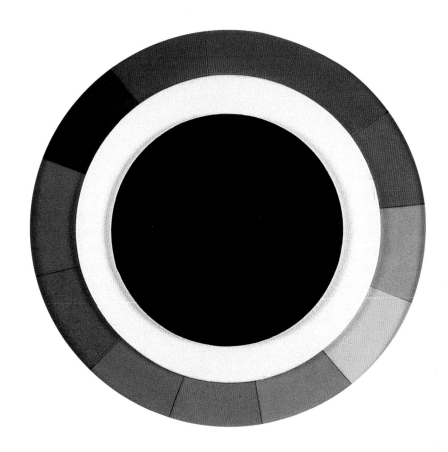

one primary color and the secondary color opposite it on the color wheel, for example, blue and orange.

Triadic. By using three colors spaced equidistant on the color wheel, such as red, blue, and yellow, triadic compositions can be formed.

In addition to following your own color preferences, ideas for creating color schemes can be derived by looking around you at colors in nature to see how they complement each other. I often refer to the colors in my flower garden or gardening catalogs when choosing a palette for my decorated papers. Look through art books, magazines, and upscale mail order

A color wheel will show you how the three primary colors—red, blue, and yellow—can be mixed to yield a host of hues.

catalogs to see what kinds of colors you prefer together. Looking at wrapping paper, wallpaper, and fabric designs can also show you pleasing color combinations.

Try making a scrapbook of color combinations you like. Let one hue dominate each page and add colored ribbons, paint chip samples, and colored paper swatches or photos cut from magazines. You'll learn about color harmony, composition, and your personal color preferences as you create your scrapbook, which is sure to be a lasting and valuable resource for all your artistic pursuits.

Understanding Design Principles

Whether layering papers and images in a collage or arranging stamped images on a piece of cover stock, you'll need to know something about how to make a unified composition to create a successful greeting card. Some stamp enthusiasts begin a card by stamping images on card stock, cutting them out, and moving them around on the card front to determine how they best integrate with the other images before committing to stamping them in specific places. Collage card artists, for sure,

spend time moving parts of the collage into different areas of the card, overlapping papers and considering horizontal and vertical orientations before deciding upon a finished composition and gluing things down.

The cards pictured in this book, many by professional designers, will give you an idea of good designs to emulate. A trip to a local card shop will also guide you; commercial cards, although lacking in texture, will usually display balanced placement of words and images. In general, it is

important to be aware of how the colors and shapes in a card design repeat, establish a rhythm, and keep your eye moving throughout the composition.

Contrasting elements keep your card from becoming boring. A corrugated or highly textured handmade paper next to a smooth one, a flash of color in an otherwise sedate monochromatic color

---

These cards by Hélène Métivier show how two different card designs can be made using the same decorative paper. Paper by Magenta.

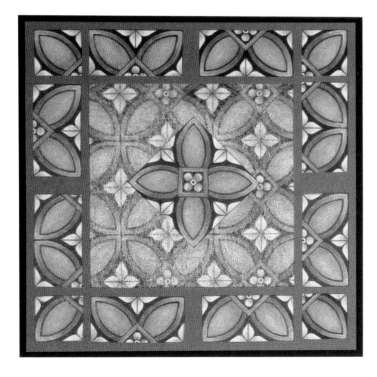

scheme, or a sharp diagonal line in the midst of horizontal ones will keep your cards exciting. The introduction of beads, buttons, metallic thread, or decorative stitching can also enliven a design. A dominant element, whether a particular shape, more intense color, or structure like a folded medallion or cast-paper addition will help unify your card design.

With a little practice and an eye to assessing what helps or hinders your compositions, you'll begin to feel more confident and uncover the reasons that some of your designs "feel" right and others, intuitively, are incomplete or overdone.

Decorative stitching on this handmade paper card by Claudia K. Lee adds a playful element to the design.

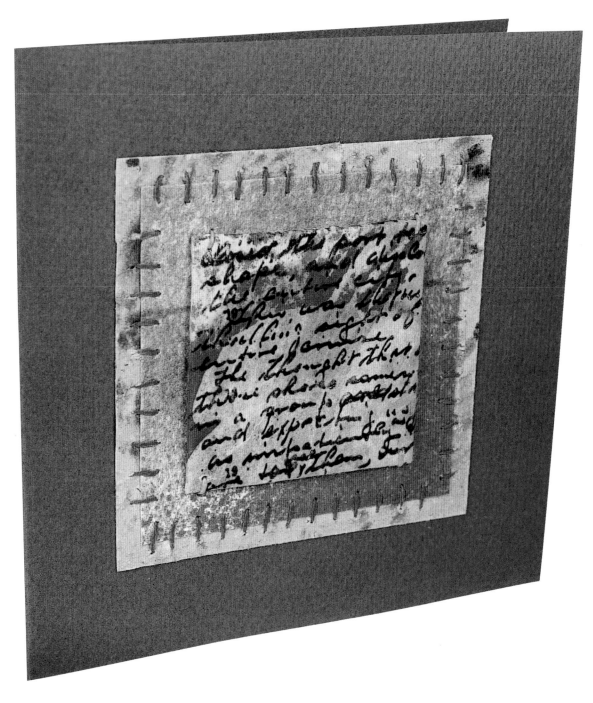

basic card-decorating
TECHNIQUES

The term "printmaking" describes many techniques that can be used to create stunning background papers for designs added over them or techniques that can be used to create the primary focal point of a card design. Everything from plastic wrap to elaborately carved linoleum block can be used to print an image on paper or fabric that can then be adhered to a card front. Many of these techniques are simple enough for a child to do, yet sophisticated-looking enough to consider using on the covers of even special-occasion cards.

Leslie Ebert created this paper for card-making by coating a sheet of Plexiglas with overlapping layers of printing ink and then placing a sheet of her handmade paper on top of the inked plate and pressing it onto the color to receive the design.

Direct Printing with Found Objects

By coating relatively flat objects with stamp pad ink or paint and then pressing them against paper or fabric, elaborate "junk prints" can be made. Flea markets, hardware stores, and what-not drawers are good places to search for printing devices. Sewing baskets, too, are good places to scour. Jane Koot coated the bases of thread spools with acrylic color and used them to create the circular designs on her card (right). Instead of printing on paper, however, Jane prints on interfacing. She prefers the density of the fabric, which she feels gives her prints a more three-dimensional appearance.

Most of the small objects used to print materials for card design can be coated with a paintbrush or pressed against a stamp pad to ink them. If you want to coat larger objects, like wire mesh, pieces of mylar, or wood blocks that can be used to print all-over designs destined to be cut down, you may want to ink a brayer or roller by rolling it over a large slow-drying stamp pad and then onto the

Spools   *JK*

Above right: Jane Koot used wooden thread spools as printing devices to create this acrylic-colored "junk print."

object. You can also coat it with paint or block-printing ink.

What You'll Need

Plexiglas or glass inking tile. This will function as a surface on which to spread the color.

Brayer or roller. Use this to spread the color on the tile and roll it onto the printing device.

Colors. Acrylic colors and water-based block-printing inks can both be used to coat larger printing devices. By avoiding oil-based products, you won't have to deal with hand protection and a complicated cleanup.

Newspapers. Newspapers will be needed to cover tabletops, absorb excess color, and create a padded printing surface when necessary.

Printing papers and fabrics. Soft block-printing papers, handmade papers, and Japanese papers such as Hosho, Moriki, and Okawara will produce fine images. Many drawing papers will also print well. Experiment to find your favorite. After you've made your print, cut and adhere it to your card stock to make your card. Try some fabrics or interfacing to see if you like them as well.

COATING THE OBJECT AND MAKING THE PRINT

Place several teaspoons of color onto the Plexiglas printing tile. Use the brayer to spread the paint or printing ink evenly by rolling in all directions. When the brayer is coated, roll it over the surface of the object you're printing to evenly disperse the color, then press the object against the paper to print it. Some rigid objects yield a better image if they're pressed against a padded surface. If an object isn't making a good print, try placing your paper on top of a newspaper pad before printing. Try repeatedly printing with one object or combine printed images on one sheet of paper. Interesting designs can also be made by letting one layer of paint dry and then printing over it

Above: The printing device Jane uses to create some of her string-print cards.

Below: String adhered to a cardboard background was used to make this card by Jane Koot.

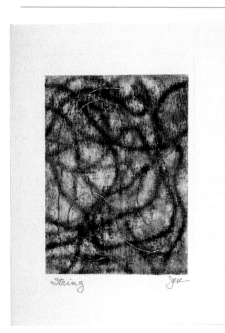

with the same object to create a double-image motif.

Create a printing block by assembling small flat objects of the same thickness and using waterproof glue to adhere them to a block of wood or other backing. Apply urethane to the printing block so it can be reused. Pieces of corrugated cardboard, string, netting, keys, pieces of rubber, mylar, puzzle pieces, etc., can create interesting prints useful in card design. Jane Koot creates string prints from her handmade printing plates and cuts decorative designs into mylar with an X-acto knife to create another type of printing device. Jane has also created a rolling printer by carving a raised leaf design into a small rolling pin.

Another way to create an all-over design that can be cut and used in your card art is to coat your Plexiglas inking plate, create a design on the plate, and then press the paper onto it, rolling over it with a dry brayer to be sure all areas of the paper make contact with the image you created. Leslie Ebert created her beautiful paper (see pages 28–29) (which she then bravely cut into sections for her cards) by brushing printing ink onto Plexiglas and transferring it onto handmade paper. Although it looks as though many separate printings would be necessary to create such a design, Leslie explains that it is one printing made by layering translucent and opaque colors, overlapping them to create new ones right on the plate surface.

Brayer Printing

The same brayer you used for the previous print-making techniques can be used to make beautiful backgrounds for card art. Debbie Tlach suggests the following techniques for using Ranger's Rainbow Rollers to create great background images.

Transfer Technique

You can ink a stamp, carved block, or other object with a stamp pad and then roll a dry brayer over the object. The brayer will pick up the design and transfer it when you roll it onto your paper. As you continue to roll, successive impressions become lighter, creating a design that fades in and out as you re-ink and roll again.

Creating Multi-colored Stripes

By inking a roller with a rainbow pad or Ranger's Big and Juicy multicolored stamp pad and then rolling it onto your paper, you can easily create a beautiful striped or plaid background image. Try re-inking your roller with darker colored inks and then using your brayer to roll partially over the first printing to create an even more interesting design. Solid color stamp pads can also be used and bands of color can overlap each other in various directions.

Creating Patterned Bands of Color

Decorate a paper like the one shown below by using linoleum block carving tools to remove parts of the roller; then ink and roll onto your paper. Alternatively, build up the surface of the roller with string, rubber bands, felt, or other materials to create patterned roller prints.

Creating Diffused Images

Try inking your roller with a rainbow multicolored stamp pad and rolling off most of the ink onto scrap paper. Next, mist the roller with water to dampen it and roll it onto your paper.

Below: A plaid background paper for card-making made by rolling a brayer over a Ranger's Big and Juicy Rainbow Pad and then onto white paper.

Opposite: Debbie Tlach inked and rolled a carved brayer onto her stamp pad and then onto coated card stock to create this background paper.

Plastic Wrap Prints

Plastic wrap can be applied to paper that has been washed with inks or diluted paints to produce various textured patterns useful as backgrounds or collage materials for your cards (see, for example, page 7).

What You'll Need

Paper. Medium- to heavy-weight watercolor paper is ideal. I like to use a watercolor block, a stack of paper bound on four sides that holds the wet paper flat until you pry it free with a dull knife. This technique makes the paper very wet, which tends to buckle as it dries. Regular watercolor paper can be used, but you may have to dampen and stretch the paper before using it.

Colors. Drawing inks, watercolors, dyes, and acrylics all work.

Color applicators. You can squirt colors on with eyedroppers or pipettes. Large watercolor brushes or foam brushes can also be used.

Spray bottle.

Plastic wrap.

Gloves (optional).

Printing Technique

Squirt or brush colored inks, dyes, or diluted paints on the surface of your paper. The colors should be quite liquid and forming puddles. Spray the colors with water to dilute them, if necessary, and move them around. You can also tilt your block of paper to encourage colors to run in a particular direction or distribute them with a very wet foam brush.

When the surface of your paper is quite wet, lay the plastic wrap over the colors. To produce a fractured pattern that resembles ice or rocks, crumple the plastic wrap first. Because you can see through it, you can rearrange it to force the wet colors into patterns until you're satisfied with the design. You can also squirt colors under the plastic wrap to create color mixtures. Pull it into long narrow bands to create landscape patterns or keep it crinkled for the look of cracked ice. When you've finished arranging the plastic wrap, weight it with a book or board to keep it in position until the colors dry. (If using acrylics, remove the wrap while the paper is still damp—the dried acrylic can act like glue.)

Squirting ink under the plastic wrap to create a multicolored plastic wrap print. While the inks are still wet, the plastic wrap can be manipulated to create a tight or loose fractured design.

Fabric and Salt Prints

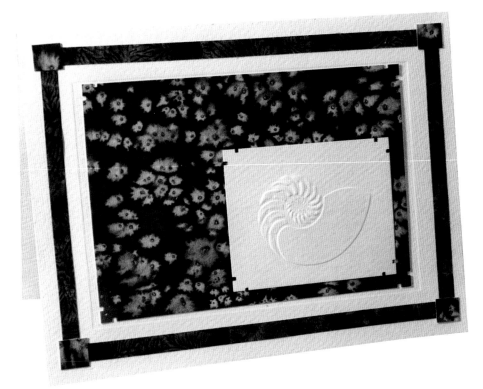

salt (table, kosher, or pretzel) is removed can suggest many things—such as a snowstorm, underwater scene, or starlit sky—depending upon what color ink you use.

WHAT YOU'LL NEED

Paper. A watercolor block or stretched watercolor paper is recommended to keep the wet paper from buckling as it dries. Other lighter weight, nonabsorbent papers can be patterned with this technique and later pressed flat.

Colors. Diluted watercolors, acrylic paints, dyes, or drawing inks.

Salt. Table salt, kosher salt, pretzel salt, etc., will produce starburst patterns of various sizes.

Color applicators. Watercolor wash brushes or foam poly brushes are used to apply the color wash.

TECHNIQUE

Apply a wash of color and immediately sprinkle on salt granules in a random or controlled manner. The pattern is more interesting if the salt granules remain distinct and aren't clumped together. Brush off the salt when the ink is thoroughly dry.

Various kinds of loosely woven fabrics and lace can also be used to make background prints for card-making. Place a piece of lace on a sheet of paper and roll over it with an inked brayer to create a kind of stencil print, or glue fabrics like netting to a board to create a direct print. Another easy way to print with fabric involves squirting or sloshing paints, inks, or dyes on a sheet of paper and then laying a piece of fabric on the wet inks. The fabric attracts the inks and leaves its imprint on the paper as it dries.

A salt print paper forms the background for this card, which also features a dry-embossed design made with a Dreamweaver stencil.

If a very liquid color wash is brushed onto a paper and salt is applied while the color is still wet, the salt will wick the color around it to produce a spotted starburst pattern when the color dries. This is an effective method of patterning background papers to use in card designs or creating an all-over design for an envelope that coordinates with the card within. The tiny mottled areas that remain after the

Leaf Printing

Tree and plant leaves have intricate detailed patterns that will be faithfully reproduced if you coat them with color and press them against paper. You can print with a single leaf or several of different sizes to decorate a card or envelope. If you live in a warm climate, you probably have a year-round supply of tree and garden plant offerings. If you live in a colder climate, you can press leaves for winter use or prune your houseplants. The leaves of many houseplants, like my parlor maple and deer's foot fern, yield great prints without any pressing.

WHAT YOU'LL NEED

A leaf-printed card and envelope by Leslie Ebert created with printers' inks.

Leaves. For the most interesting prints, select fresh leaves with textured surfaces and veins running through them. Fern, geranium, maple, and ginkgo leaves are favorites for making prints on greeting cards. Smooth glossy leaves will usually print as disappointing solid shapes, although they may work as background prints for leaves printed over them. Be sure you are able to recognize poison oak and ivy before you embark on your leaf-hunting expedition.

Plant press. A city telephone directory will work as well. This flattens the leaves and removes some of their moisture. Leave a few pages between specimens. If you live in a small town, your phone book may not be heavy enough— add a few books to weigh it down.

Plexiglas sheet. Use this as a leaf-inking plate.

Colors. Water-based colors and acrylic paints can be used to coat the leaf. Ink pads and brush markers are also good choices.

Color applicators. Small watercolor brushes, raised foam stamp pads, and soft rubber rollers or brayers can be used to coat the leaf with color. The brushes can also be used for color mixing.

Tweezers (optional). These will be helpful for picking up the inked leaf and placing it in position on the printing paper.

Paper. Drawing, Oriental, watercolor, printmaking, and handmade papers will yield fine prints. Inexpensive bond paper also works quite well. Many card artists prefer

to print on a soft textured paper and then mount it on coordinating card stock. Others prefer to print directly on the folded card.

Newspaper and scrap paper. Newspapers can be used to protect working surfaces. Scrap paper will protect your fingers from ink when making the print.

INKING THE LEAF

If you're working with acrylics, place a small amount of paint on the Plexiglas and use a brayer to roll it out. Carefully roll the inked brayer over the flattened leaf to deposit a thin layer of color on its entire surface. Too much paint will create a print with fuzzy edges; too little will yield an incomplete image. Experiment to learn how much paint to apply. If using watercolor paints or brush markers, coat the leaf as evenly as possible, creating color blends if desired. If using a raised stamp pad, press the pad against the leaf.

MAKING THE PRINT

Use tweezers or your fingers to gently lift the leaf and deposit it, color side down, on the printing paper. Roll over it with a clean brayer or cover it with a piece of scrap paper and use your fingers to gently rub it down. When all parts of the leaf have made contact with the printing paper, lift the leaf up and set it aside to ink again for another print.

Above: Rubbing the back of a leaf to deposit color and create another leaf print on a paper destined to be made into greeting cards.

Left: A leaf-printed card by Fred B. Mullett.

Create different types of images on your cards and envelopes by varying the sizes of the leaves you use and the amount of ink or paint you apply to each leaf so the images fade in and out. Print several leaves in shades of the same hue or mix your colors to create color blends directly on the leaf.

Fred Mullett creates leaf-printed cards (above left) that he describes more as "diffused watercolor impressions of leaves" rather than "prints." As he explains, "These were done with very wet watercolors brushed directly onto the plant and then placed onto the paper. I also might take a brush with water or pale pigmentation and 'fill in' some of the leaf shapes. When dry, certain areas of the image were highlighted with markers and fine-tipped colored pens."

$\mathcal{R}$ubber Stamping

Without a doubt, the most popular tool for creating a handcrafted card is the rubber stamp. Literally millions are available from hundreds of stamp companies, with images that run from cute to x-rated. You won't find either in this book, but you will see many others that are amazing in their detail and breadth of subject matter. Stamps can be purchased to convey all types of wishes and emotions. Images and words abound that allow almost anyone to produce a beautiful or esoteric greeting in record time.

Stamp artists like Lea Everse and Fred Mullett take stamp art a bit further. The quality of many of their works approaches fine art. Several of their techniques, as well as those by other stamp artists, will be explored elsewhere in this chapter. Instructions are also given for those purists who prefer to carve their own stamps.

WHAT YOU'LL NEED

Rubber stamp. A purchased stamp or one you've cut yourself.

Coloring agents. Raised stamp pads in a range of solid, rainbow (with several bands or blocks of color in one pad), and metallic colors should go in your stamping tool box. Water-based brush pens are great for creating color blends on your stamps.

Clear embossing pad. To deposit colorless ink on your stamp for thermal embossing.

Embossing powders. Use a range of colors to create raised thermal embossed designs.

Embossing heat tool. Use this to melt the embossing powders.

Paper. Almost any type will do, although some unsized handmade papers will yield soft-edged images if stamped with water-based inks. Stamp directly on your card stock or envelope, or stamp on a textured paper that you can layer with others on your folded card.

INKING THE STAMP

To use a stamp pad properly, press your stamp against it with just enough force to deposit ink on the raised design. If you press too hard, you'll ink the background of the stamp or the base that holds it.

To use a raised stamp pad, press it against the stamp to deposit ink. Many raised pads like those by Colorbox come in sets of related colors, making it easy to coordinate colors if you're new to card-making. Because many of these are narrow pads, they can be used for making color blends on one stamp. Most raised pads also come in a larger format for inking large stamps so you can cover a wider area.

My favorite tools for applying color to rubber stamps are watercolor brush pens. Sections of the stamp can be inked in various colors and beautiful color blends are easily created. One problem, how-

ever, is that if you get too involved with creating the perfect color blend, parts of the stamp can begin to dry prematurely. By exhaling onto your stamp just before using it, you can usually re-moisten drying areas.

Because metallic markers and some opaque pigment inks tend to dry more slowly, you can use them at a more leisurely pace. Be aware though, that some of these take hours to dry and can smear if you continue working on the card you've recently stamped them on.

MAKING THE PRINT

To begin stamping, press your inked stamp against your paper firmly, without rocking it. Rotate the stamp to create variations on a

A multilayered stamped and handpainted card by Lea Everse. Image by Stonehouse Stamps.

repetitive design. Sophisticated border designs for cards and matching envelopes can be made by alternating stamp designs or by stamping in one color and then restamping over the initial image in a related color or a metallic ink, slightly offsetting the first image. Extra long narrow stamps that easily span the length of a card or envelope are also available for making border designs.

For stamped images that resemble watercolor paintings, ink your stamp with water-based inks and then dampen it with a fine mist from a spray bottle before stamping.

Opposite: Long rubber stamps like these by JudiKins (top and center) and Rubber Stampede, Inc. (bottom) are great for making border designs.

THERMAL EMBOSSED IMAGES

By applying embossing powder to a wet stamped image and then heating and melting the powder, you can create a raised design to add dimension to your cards. Powders are available in an array of solid, metallic, and pearlescent colors. Clear embossing powder is also available to highlight colors stamped beneath them, giving stamped images or words a wet, glossy look. The powders can be melted by holding the stamped and powdered sheet of paper over an iron or a lightbulb, but these methods usually take a long time to melt the powder and sometimes result in scorched papers. It makes good sense to visit your local craft store to buy an embossing heat tool created for melting embossing powders. This will make embossing much easier.

To emboss an image, first coat your stamp with a slow-drying ink.

It is easiest to use clear ink pads if you plan to cover the stamped image with a single color embossing powder. Stamp your image on the paper or card and sprinkle the embossing powder over it. Shake the paper to spread the powder over the stamped image, then shake the excess powder onto a piece of folded paper so that it can be easily returned to the bottle. Use a cotton swab or small brush to wipe away any powder that's clinging to parts of the paper you don't intend to emboss. Next, heat the powder (from above, if using an embossing heat tool) to melt it and create the embossed image.

If the image you want to thermal emboss is large or if you are doing a number of embossed cards at one time, it may be easier if you fill a bowl with embossing powder and just drag your still wet stamped card through it to coat the stamped area quickly.

Above: Melting the gold embossing powder with an embossing heat tool. The stamped butterfly image is by Magenta.

Left: A suminagashi and paste-painted card with a thermal-embossed Celtic knot decoration.

"Painting with Plastic"

Fred Mullet creates beautiful embossed images for his cards. His painting background led him to experiment with thermal embossing in a new way, using a spot application of colored embossing powders over an initial multicolored stamped image. The result is a miniature painting with gradations of color and value that give it a three-dimensional look. Fred describes his technique, used to create the image shown:

"The rubber stamp of a fish image was inked in two colors of pigment-based ink: scarlet red toward the top and light gray toward the bottom. These two separate colorings were blended into each other to create a print that has a stronger color and darker value on the top portion of the image.

"A transparent orange embossing powder was sprinkled lightly and sparsely over the top half of the print and a clear embossing powder was lightly sprinkled over the bottom half. These two areas were then blended together by lightly shaking the card stock. This creates a steady transition from one color to the other rather than hard-edged areas of difference. The excess was tapped off and the image then heated with a craft heat tool. The print, with its change in

color and value coupled with the blend of transparent powders, now creates an embossed image that moves from red through red-orange through orange and on into gray. Very effective in its own right, but we're not done yet.

"A base-gradated color wash was then applied to the image. Since embossing powders are essentially plastic and generally resistant to water media, this watercolor foundation slides down into the 'valleys' of paper between the 'mountains' of

The gradations of color and value in Fred B. Mullet's thermal-embossed images make his cards look more like miniature paintings than rubber-stamped designs.

melted powder. This has the potential to create areas of color and contrast that range from sublime to outrageous!

"After the base watercolor had dried, further accents and highlighting were done with water-based markers and more watercolor."

*U*sing Household Bleach to Create Stamped Images

Rubber stamps can be used to create an image by removing color from a paper's surface as well as being used to deliver color. Although Fred Mullett uses this technique primarily to ready an image for additional painting on dark paper, I find the bleached images beautiful without further coloring. This technique is not for those interested in producing archival works, however, as the bleach will eat through the paper eventually. The following technique describes Fred's process.

TECHNIQUE

1. Household bleach was brushed onto a rubber stamp of a fish. The rubber and bleach were then sprayed with water and placed onto the black paper. (Be forewarned, not all black paper bleaches out. Individual tests need to be made.) The stamp was lifted, sprayed again, and placed in another location. The bleach begins to be spent with each application, hence the images will seem to fade into the background. This process of creating diffuse, nonspecific images is continued until the composition is finished, creating the foundation that will be the background (see above).

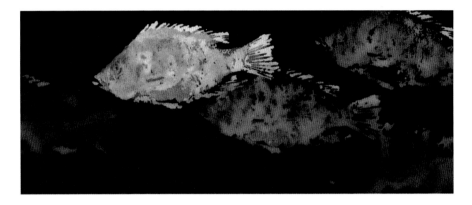

2. Having this series of images that has been bleached lighter than the black paper, it is now easier to color in these areas with transparent pigments with watercolor or markers (opposite, top).

3. Highly pigmented, opaque color is now applied to the rubber stamp and aligned over the main image in the composition. This ink should be lighter in value than the colored images beneath, appearing to come forward even more dramatically than the diffused images that make up the background (opposite, center).

4. Further highlighting and fine tuning the color on the main image makes it really stand out. Complementary coloring is used, but is subordinate to the idea of shaping the image with value and value contrasts. After applying the Chinese seal and signing, the

Above and opposite: Fred B. Mullett used a rubber stamp dipped in bleach to remove color from black paper to create a series of images that were painted with transparent pigments. An opaque pigment with a lighter value than the colored images beneath it was next stamped over the main image to create a card design with considerable depth.

paper is trimmed to size and glued to the card stock (opposite, bottom). This format is designed for use in a #10 business size envelope. Fred usually writes a letter and folds it to fit inside this presentation.

Note: When working with bleach, Fred has found that black envelopes from Astrobright bleach out well. He noted that Arches Black Cover (a printmaking paper) works well, but has a bit too much texture to yield a fine stamp print. Hammermill Via Black in a card stock weight is another paper he recommends for bleaching.

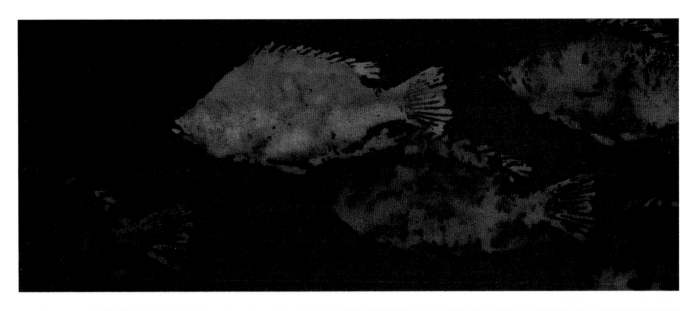

$\mathcal{U}$sing Masking Techniques

$\mathcal{M}$asking allows a card artist to stamp images over each other without disturbing the previous images. By using masking techniques, the image stamped first can remain in the foreground of your card while images stamped over it appear in the background. The result is a card displaying more dimension, rather than one with images simply stamped next to each other. To create his card (below), Fred Mullett stamped his large fish image, stamped the fish again on a piece of scrap paper, then cut it out and placed it over the previously stamped fish to shield it from the red and orange geometric shapes stamped next.

Masking can be used another way to simply preserve a large area from further stamping. Lea Everse's envelope (opposite) was stamped with a red leaf design, after which the horizontal address area was masked off so that a second layer of black and a third layer of gold stamping could be added to select areas of the envelope.

Opposite, top: Lea Everse's envelope with the mask in place. Notice how the mask prevents the third layer of gold stamping from reaching the address area of the envelope.

Opposite, below: Lea's finished envelope with the mask removed. The mask has prevented both the black and the gold stamped foliage from appearing in the enter of the envelope. Rubber stamp by Stamps in Motion.

Below: Fred B. Mullett used masking techniques to create this card, in which the image stamped first remains in the foreground while the images stamped afterward appear in the background.

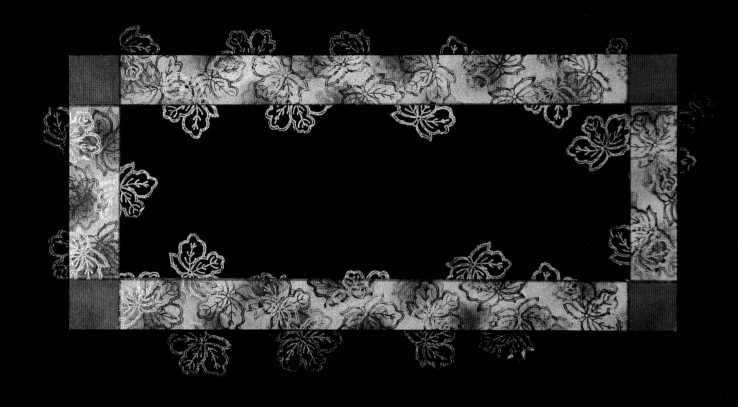

Diane Maurer
Post Office Box Number 78
Spring Mills, PA 16875·0078

Creating Raised Stamped Cutouts

A card with lots of dimension, like that by Lea Everse (below), can be created by stamping an image and coloring, thermal embossing, or otherwise decorating the stamped image and then carefully cutting it out and setting it aside. When the folded card has been similarly decorated, a piece of double-sided foam tape can be cut and affixed to the back of the stamped cutout.

The cutout can then be pressed in place on the finished card to create an image that floats above the rest of the card's surface.

There's a lot of room for a card artist to create an original

composition in her or his own unique style by layering papers and using other techniques, even though they may use purchased stamps to create the images. If you are a purist who likes to work from scratch or simply want to try your hand at carving a stamp, read on.

What You'll Need

Carving material. A Mars-Staedtler Plastic Grand Eraser, Pink Pearl, or other large eraser can be carved easily. For making larger stamps, Safety-Kut, a very soft linoleum-like material, is great.

Carving tools. An X-acto knife with #11 blades and a linoleum cutter with V-blades of various sizes make good carving tools.

Pencil. A soft pencil is useful for drawing designs on the eraser or tracing designs from other sources.

Tracing paper.

Optional equipment. An alcohol-soaked cotton ball can be used to remove printed logos from erasers

Above right: Kimberly Byerly carved her own stamps to create this scarab card.

Opposite: Lea Everse stamped and cut out the flower on this paste paper card so she could elevate it from the background with a piece of foam tape. Flower image by Stamp Affair.

and transfer photocopied images from source material.

Choosing a Design

The first step in carving your own stamp is choosing and transferring a design to your carving material. Clip-art books, illustrations from magazines and newspapers, computer-generated drawings, or your own drawings can all become rubber-stamped designs. Looking at wrapping paper and fabric designs can often yield ideas for pattern stamps that you can use to create borders or background images on your cards.

Transferring the Design

Use alcohol and a cotton ball to remove any printed logo from the eraser and cut the eraser or Safety-Kut to an appropriate size. Next, use a pencil or pen to draw directly on your eraser, bearing in mind that what you draw will print in reverse. If you trace a design from source material or work out your own drawing on tracing paper you can invert your tracing onto the eraser and rub the back of the image with your fingernail or a coin to transfer it to the eraser.

Images can be photocopied to enlarge or reduce them and then transferred to your carving material. Lay the photocopy face-down on the eraser and rub the back of it with a cotton ball soaked in alcohol to transfer the design. Touch up the design with a pencil or pen if necessary.

Cutting a Sketched Design

Once you have clear lines to follow, you can begin cutting away the unwanted material around your design. Push the V-shaped linoleum cutter away from you to remove parts of the carving material, remembering to keep the printing surface level. The X-acto knife is handy for cutting fine

Using a linoleum cutter to create Kimberly Byerly's scarab stamp. Beginning carvers will find it easier and safer to allow more material to remain around the image they're carving.

detailed areas and trimming away borders.

Always make sure you cut away from your image so there's enough material remaining under it to support it for repeated stamping. Work slowly, inking and stamping as you cut to make sure you're cutting deeply enough and removing the parts you intend to. Remember, you can always make another cut, but you can't reattach eraser or Safety-Kut parts removed in error.

tenciling

By applying color through an opening cut in heavy paper, acetate, or a brass plate, you can produce beautiful stenciled designs to decorate your greeting cards and envelopes. Lynell Harlow, owner of Dream-weaver Stencils, produces an extensive line of brass stenciling and embossing plates that make stenciling a snap. Because you can often combine images using several of her stencils to create your own designs, you needn't feel guilty about not starting from scratch.

If you prefer to create your own stencil, however, you can purchase translucent stencil acetate, trace or draw designs on it, and use an X-acto knife to cut openings through which to apply your color. Pre-cut stencils can be purchased and examined to see how the bridge—the solid piece of acetate that separates parts of a design—helps to define a silhouette.

WHAT YOU'LL NEED

Color applicators. Stencil brushes with natural bristles cut to the same length can be used for applying colors. For detailed small areas, it's handy to have small color applicators. To begin, three brushes ⅛" to ½" in diameter are good.

A stenciled card by Elaine Benedict. Elaine blended her colors and applied them with a lighter touch in some areas to give the vase dimension. Stencils by Dreamweaver.

Paper towels. These will be used to remove excess color from your brushes and stencils.

Paper. Just about any text-weight paper or card stock can be stenciled.

Stenciling colors. Creamy stencil paints, stenciling chalks, and water-soluble pigment ink pads like those made by Tsukineko work well and eliminate the bleed under the stencil that may occur with liquid colors. Most ink and dye pads used for rubber stamping can be used as long as you remember to tap off most of the color so you are working with an almost-dry brush.

Two methods of applying stencil paint include stippling—tapping the perpendicular brush on the stencil opening until it has been covered with color—and rouging. Rouging is done by moving the almost-dry brush in a circular motion (like doing the hula!), rubbing the paint into the stencil openings. Work on top of the acetate or brass plate at first, moving from the edge of the opening to its center, laying down a thin layer of color.

It's not necessary to fill in the entire stencil opening with intense color. A darker shading on the edges of the opening leading to a lighter concentration of color in the center of a design is more beautiful than a flat solid-colored design and will often make designs look dimensional.

Colors can be mixed and blended together to create different hues as you stencil your card. Lynell suggests that you always start out stenciling with the lightest colors first, followed by the medium and finally the darkest ones. She recommends using three brushes: one for yellows; the second for reds and oranges; and the third for blues, greens, and purples. When switching colors on each of these brushes (going from blue to green, for instance), you can just rub out the unwanted color on a paper towel and load your brush with the next color.

APPLYING COLOR

Begin using removable tape to secure your cut stencil in position over your folded card or envelope. (A brass stencil can sometimes simply be held in place, but it's safer to tape it, too.) To charge your brush with color, hold it perpendicular and just touch the surface of the color container with the flat bristles of the stencil brush. Then, still holding your brush perpendicular, tap it against a paper towel to evenly distribute the color. The brush should be almost dry when it's used, to prevent the color from creeping under the stencil openings and blurring the edges of your designs.

FINISHING

After applying color through your stencil, pick the stencil straight up so as not to disturb the design. Wipe off any color before it dries. If you're doing repeat designs, to be used as background images on cards, be sure that your stencils are free of color before moving them to another position on your card.

USING EMBOSSING PASTE WITH BRASS STENCILS

Instead of adding color through your stencil openings, you can apply Dreamweaver's embossing paste to create a raised design. The look is different than the raised thermographic embossing created with embossing powders in that it has a distinctly crisp edge. To use this embossing paste, work on a hard flat surface and tape your stencil down on your card all around with wide removable tape. The tape will hold the stencil in place as well as shield your paper from any embossing paste that may go beyond the edges of your brass stencil as you apply it. Next, pick up some embossing paste on the bottom of a palette knife and smooth it over the stencil's openings as though you are icing a cake or applying spackle.

When all the openings in the stencil are filled, scrape off the excess paste so that the stencil surface is smooth. The paste on the stencil will be $\frac{1}{8}$" to $\frac{1}{4}$" thick. Now it's time to remove the tape (easiest if you start with the piece applied last) and carefully pull the stencil straight up. Immediately clean off the stencil with a nailbrush and water or drop it in a dish of water so the paste doesn't dry on the brass. The embossing

Smoothing translucent embossing paste mixed with Ranger's Perfect Pearls metallic powder into the openings of a brass stencil. When it dries it will look like the sun image on the card pictured.

paste on your card will dry in about 30 minutes. When it dries, you can put the stencil back in place and apply color again, using iridescent paint sticks or metallic ink pads for a vibrant shine.

USING TRANSLUCENT EMBOSSING PASTE

Translucent embossing paste can also be applied through a stencil to give a glossy translucent finish to your cards. It can be mixed with iridescent powders or metallic acrylic paints to create greetings that glow. Usually about a $\frac{1}{2}$ teaspoon of powder or paint can be mixed into 2 tablespoons of paste with good results.

$\mathcal{D}$ry Embossing

Those beautiful raised flowers, ornate borders, and decorative designs commonly seen on wedding invitations will be easy to create on your own cards, using a technique called dry embossing. Embossing creates a raised area on a piece of paper that looks quite elegant. Embossing on white paper looks particularly beautiful when light and shadow accentuate the designs.

Dry Embossing with Stenciling Plates

The brass plates used for stenciling can also be used as embossing plates to create raised designs on your cards and envelopes. Art papers, handmade papers, and cover- and text-weight papers used on your cards can all be embossed, provided you can see through them when a light source shines from behind. A ball-tipped burnisher, available at any craft supply shop, will allow you to reproduce detailed designs, including elaborate Celtic knots and ornate borders, with tiny areas that would be practically impossible to cut by hand.

To use a brass stencil for embossing, place the stencil on the front of the paper you wish to emboss. If you're embossing a folded card, check to make sure that the raised embossing will appear right-side up on the front of the card. Use a piece of removable tape to hold the stenciling/embossing plate in place, then invert the paper and stencil and place the paper stencil-side-down on a light box or against a sunny window.

Working on the back of the paper, use a ball burnisher to press the paper into the illuminated opening. Move the burnisher around the edge of the cutout until a crisp pattern appears. It's not necessary to burnish the center of the opening—just running your burnisher around the edges will lift the whole design. Turn the stencil and attached paper as you work if necessary to reach all parts of the design. Be sure to leave the paper attached to the stencil until you're positive you've completely embossed it. Once you've moved the stencil, it's practically impossible to get it back into position.

If you use a paper with a bumpy texture or "tooth" like Canson Mi-Teintes and many other art papers, you may find that the embossing tool tends to drag as you move it. You can remedy the situation by rubbing the ball burnisher on a piece of waxed paper to help it glide more easily.

If you wish to add color to your embossed design, leave the stencil in place and use stenciling brushes to add color to the work.

Moving the ball-tipped burnisher around the edge of the opening in the brass stencil to raise the embossed design.

Spraying, Spattering, and Sponging Techniques

Spraying, spattering, and sponging techniques are very simple to master and great for creating background designs for cards and envelopes. You can spatter, sponge, and spray through a brass or hand-cut stencil or through other found objects with openings such as plastic rug backings, doilies, radiator screens, etc.

You can also scatter objects like leaves, plastic photographic slide mounts, washers, etc., and add color around them to decorate paper. Spatter with one color, let the paint dry, and then move the objects to another position and spray again. Shades of the same or different colors can be used.

SPATTERING TECHNIQUES

Thin acrylic paint with water or use drawing inks or fabric dyes and spatter the colors on with low-tech tools—a vegetable brush and tongue depressor. Just place some paint or ink in a flat dish, coat the brush with color, and tap off some of the paint. Then, with bristles up and the front of the brush tipped downward, draw the tongue depressor toward you to spatter paint on your paper. If you're working inside, you may want to spatter inside a cardboard box to avoid decorating the entire room.

For neater and more consistent size spatters, try using the Speckling Brush made by Loew-Cornell. To operate this tool, coat the brush tips with paint and then turn a handle to rotate the brush against a metal pin. The paint will spatter in the direction in which you turn the handle.

Spattered papers like this one by Claudia K. Lee make great background paper for cards.

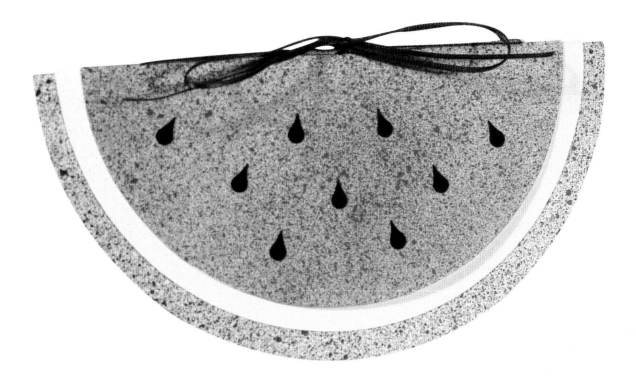

USING SPRAY WEBBING

Spray webbing, available in several colors in most craft stores, can also be used effectively to decorate a card, envelope, or piece of paper to be folded into a card. Practice using spray webbing by beginning to spray off the paper and then moving over the paper with a sweeping motion, letting the webbing fall onto the paper as you pass over it.

Above: Acrylic paint was spattered on paper circles, which were then folded in half to create this pamphlet-stitched watermelon-shaped card.

Right: Layers of spray webbing were colored with foils and embossing enamels while the spray web was still wet in this card by Suze Weinberg. A tiny book and an image cast in Ultra Thick Embossing Enamel adds to the decoration.

Left: Lea Everse used a Letra Jet airbrush tool and paper masks to create a vibrant waved design on this envelope.

Below: Cathy Rogge made successive sponge prints and then stamped over them to create this First Day Cover envelope. Stamp by Postmodern Design.

AIRBRUSH TECHNIQUES

An airbrush can be used to spray a fine color mist to create a background for your cards and envelopes. Another, less-expensive version of the airbrush—the blitzer—can be used to create a similar effect. By squeezing the bulb of the blitzer, air is forced out onto the tip of a color marker, propelling inks onto your paper. Alcohol-based markers seem to work best with this tool. Lee Everse makes incredible waved designs for her envelopes with a similar tool; they serve as the perfect background for her calligraphy.

Paper masks may be used to define an area to be sprayed or air brushed. To create subtle or vibrant backgrounds for your cards and envelopes, try tearing or cutting paper in gentle hill-and-valley shapes and spattering or spraying over it in different colors as you move it into position.

SPONGED DESIGNS

Sponges are also useful for creating card and envelope designs. Use an assortment—from makeup to sea sponges—with various size openings, and tap them against stamp pads or dip them in paints, inks, or dyes to load them with color. Blot some of the color off on a paper towel before you begin sponging, then apply color through openings in a stencil, over a paper mask, or by using the sponge at random to add texture, pattern, and color to cards and envelopes. If you cut off hard edges on sponges, you can round their corners to produce a softer design.

Making successive sponge prints by sponging with one color, letting it dry, and continuing with another (working from light to dark) will create interesting color blends and produce vivid designs like Cathy Rogge's stunning envelope (opposite). Sponges can also be used to create texture by leaving their imprint as they remove color, as shown on Suze Weinberg's card (below). Suze spritzed a glossy card with water and let ink from metallic markers flow onto the wet surface to begin a background design, then blotted the wet inks with sponges to lift color and create texture before continuing with stamping and further embellishment.

Wet sponges can be used to create texture by leaving their imprint as they lift color, as shown in this card by Suze Weinberg.

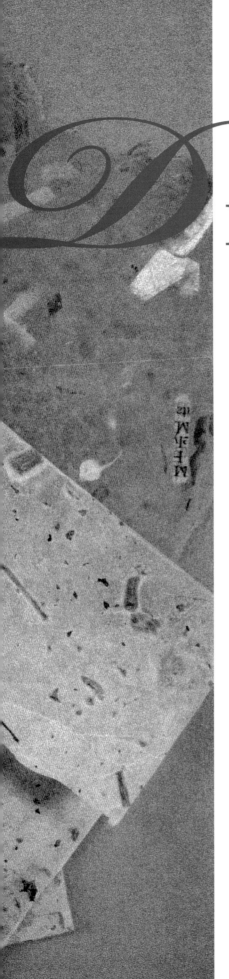

creating handmade and
ECORATIVE
papers for card design

By learning some simple techniques for making and decorating your own paper, you'll add considerably to your card-making options. Suminagashi, chalk, and bubble-marbled papers, paste papers, and batik designs can be layered with other papers to produce a gorgeous card or can be used alone as the decorative panel on a folded card to produce a sophisticated greeting or announcement. Handmade papers can, likewise, be folded to become the background for other papers layered atop them or be created with flower petals and other additions that produce a greeting that needs no further embellishment. What fun it is for a friend to receive a handmade paper card containing bits of colorful foreign currency or pieces of the road map you used on a trip together to Costa Rica!

Multicolor shredded papers and seeds create delightful inclusions in these handmade paper envelopes by Claudia K. Lee.

Creating Handmade Paper

Although domestic and imported handmade papers in every imaginable color and texture are readily available for making greeting cards and envelopes, it's really rewarding to make your own paper. The transformation of fibers swirling around in a blender into an actual piece of paper is something of a miracle and being a part of it is wonderful! Because materials and equipment are inexpensive and papermaking is so easy, anyone interested in card design should have stores of their own handmade papers to choose from.

Layered, spattered, stamped, and stitched handmade papers form a decorative panel for the front of this card by Claudia K. Lee.

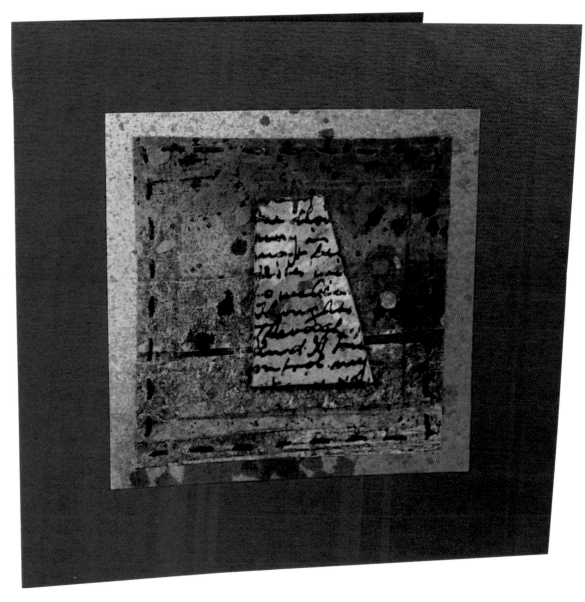

What You'll Need

Kitchen blender. You'll need a basic blender for macerating the fiber to make the paper pulp. Purchase one that you can reserve for papermaking only.

Large dishpan or plastic storage container. Either of these can serve as a papermaking vat. It should be about 8" deep and large enough to accommodate the mold and deckle with room to spare.

Mold and deckle. The mold is the screened frame that the newly formed sheet of paper rests on. The deckle rests on top of the mold to keep the pulp in place. The mold and matching deckle determine the size and shape of the sheet of paper made. Purchase a set through one of the papermaking houses.

Sponges. These are used for cleanup and to help release uncooperative sheets from the mold.

Couching cloths. These are used to support newly formed sheets of paper. Non-adhesive Pellon from a fabric store or old cotton sheets will serve this purpose. These should be approximately 2" larger all around than the paper you intend to make. Handi Wipes can also be used if you don't mind the slight pattern they impart to the paper. You can also couch on highly textured fabric to deliberately impart texture to your card materials.

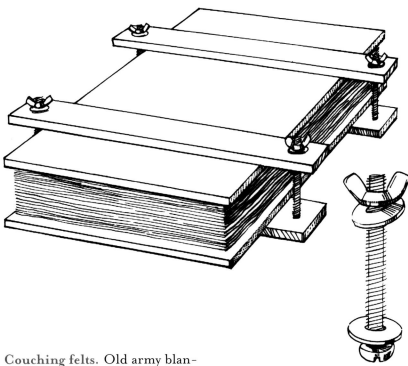

Couching felts. Old army blankets or purchased felts will support and help draw water from the wet stack of papers. These should be about 2" inches larger all around than the papers you make.

Pressing boards. You'll need two of these, made from formica or urethaned wood. They should be slightly larger than your paper mold. They will sandwich your post or stack of couched sheets and, with the help of some weight placed atop them, remove most of the water from your newly formed sheets of paper. A paper press is easy to make (above) and is an efficient way to press a stack of wet paper.

Strainer and mesh curtain material. Use these to strain out the extra pulp at the end of your papermaking session and store it for later use.

A paper press consisting of two press boards, four strips of waterproofed wood, and bolts with wing nuts can be used to apply pressure to a stack of wet papers.

Furnish. This is the raw material from which the paper is made. It can come from several sources:

Sheets of pulp. Abaca (from banana leaf fibers) or cotton linters (pulp in sheet form) can be ordered from papermaking supply houses. These are easy to use, and produce fine papers.

Recycled paper. Computer paper, photocopy paper, old blotters, pieces of drawing paper, mountboard, etc., can all be used to make handmade paper. Newspapers and magazines should be avoided as they are highly acidic.

Water. Sometimes mineral or organic compounds in water will cause brown stains to appear in a dried sheet. Use purified or distilled water for papermaking if you have high levels of minerals like iron, copper, or manganese in your tap water.

Inclusions. Decorative additions like dried flowers, bits of ribbon, mica particles, or threads can be added to the vat and stirred so they float randomly before making a sheet of paper. They can also be added while pulping, although the flowers will no longer remain whole and long threads may snarl the blender.

Sizing. Liquid sizing, from a papermaking supplier, can be added to your pulp to make sheets less absorbent. This will be important if you want to letter directly on the handmade paper on your cards. An alternative is to size your dried sheets by dissolving one teaspoon of gelatin in one cup of boiling water and painting it on with a soft, wide brush.

Pigments and retention aid. For vibrant, permanently colored papers, order pigments and retention aid (to help the pigments bond to the paper fibers) from a papermaking supplier. Follow the instructions from the supplier to use them. You can also add colored papers or use fabric dyes to color your pulp.

PREPARING THE PULP

There are two options for preparing the pulp for handmade paper, depending on your pulp source.

Using linters. Wet several linters and tear them into 1" pieces. Add a small handful of torn linters to a blender ⅔ full of warm water. The general rule is to use about 1 part linter to 2 parts warm water. Beat for about 1 minute, using short bursts of speed to avoid straining the blender motor.

Empty the blended pulp into your papermaking vat and add approximately 2 more blendersful of water. Continue beating and pouring into your vat, adding additional water each time, until you have approximately 1 pint con-centrated pulp mixed with 4 gallons of water. You needn't be too concerned with exact proportions. The ratio of pulp to water can be adjusted to create thinner or thicker sheets by adding more water or concentrated pulp to your vat.

Using recycled papers. Light- to medium-weight papers should be torn into 1" pieces and soaked overnight. Heavy watercolor paper needs to be torn into smaller pieces and soaked for several days. For very heavy paper or mount-board, even longer soaking times or boiling may be necessary. Lightweight papers will probably need to be beaten for 15 seconds or so, while heavier materials will have to be macerated longer to adequately separate the fibers.

USING A MOLD AND DECKLE TO FORM A SHEET

Use your hand to stir and distribute the pulp throughout the water in your vat. Place your deckle on top of the screened side of your mold so that the flat edges are together. Hold the deckle in place with your thumbs and grasp the mold underneath with your fingers. If your mold is rectangular, place your hands in position on the short sides.

Hold the mold and deckle at a slight angle and lower them into the vat at the far edge. Then bring the mold and deckle toward you, shifting them to a horizontal position and holding them level for a moment just below the water's surface before lifting them swiftly up and out of the vat.

As the water drains through the screen, gently shake the mold and deckle from side to side and from front to back to disperse and mesh the pulp fibers you've scooped up. When most of the water has drained back into the vat, tilt the mold and deckle slightly to let additional excess water drain off. Now rest your mold and deckle on the edge of the vat and carefully remove the deckle, making sure you don't drip water on your newly formed sheet of paper.

If you do accidentally drip water, creating a thin spot or a hole in your sheet, or if your first sheet appears too thick or thin in one area, place the mold pulp-side-down on the surface of the pulp and water slurry to "kiss off" the sheet back into the vat.

You'll soon master the smooth, continuous motion that produces a uniform sheet of paper. Judging how much pulp to add to the water in your vat will also come with experience. In general, if your paper seems too thick, add more water to the vat. If it's too thin (as it will become when you've made several sheets), add more beaten pulp to it.

Leslie Ebert lifting her mold and deckle from the papermaking vat.

COUCHING

After you've removed the deckle from the mold it's time to couch (rhymes with "pooch") the sheet. Couching refers to transferring the newly formed sheet of paper from the mold to the dampened cloth or felt. Your felts and couching cloths should be about 2" inches larger all around than your paper. To prepare a couching pad, place a dampened felt on your urethaned press board and place another dampened piece of cotton fabric or interfacing on top of the felt. Smooth out any wrinkles in the cloths (unless you want textured sheets) and then stand your mold upright at the edge of the cloth and roll the mold firmly down. When the opposite edge of the mold makes contact with the cloth, lift the first edge up. Usually the slight rocking motion releases the sheet of paper. (If you have difficulty getting the paper to let go at first, place the mold face-down on the couching cloth and use a wet sponge to press and release the back of the sheet through the mold screen.)

When the sheet is successfully couched (a French term meaning

---

Leslie Ebert couching her newly formed sheet of paper onto a textured couching cloth. The texture of the cloth will impart an embossed design on the handmade paper. To create smooth sheets of paper, use an untextured couching cloth and smooth out any wrinkles.

"to lay down"), dampen another couching cloth (if you are making another smooth paper) and place it on top of the wet sheet of paper. Your next piece of handmade paper will be couched on top of this cloth. To build up a stack or post of papers, continue couching and adding dampened cloths until you've created a stack of about 10 sheets. Then add another thick felt to the top of the stack and cover with the other press board.

Above: Using a wet sponge to help release the pulp from the mold.

Left: Removing the mold from the couched sheet.

Creating Handmade and Decorative Papers for Card Design 65

Pressing

If you don't have a paper press, the simplest way to press out the water from your post of papers is to stand on the top press board for about ten minutes to press out most of the water and then lay a couple of bricks on top of the board to finish the job.

C-clamps can also be placed on the stack and tightened to press out moisture. Regardless of which pressing method you choose, if you're not outside or near a floor drain, be sure to elevate the post of papers in a larger tub or kitty litter pan to allow the water to drain away.

Drying

When most of the moisture has been pressed out of your hand-made papers, you can transfer them to a flat drying surface like glass, Plexiglas, or formica. Transport each sheet on its couching cloth and use a wide, flat brush to gently brush the back of

---

Leslie Ebert wrinkled a cloth and then couched on top of it to create paper for the card shown. She used an airbrush to color the white handmade paper after it was dry.

the cloth to coax the sheet onto the drying surface. Then peel off the couching cloth. Allow the sheet to remain in position until completely dry.

With the damp sheet attached, you can also pin each couching cloth to Styrofoam or urethaned wood to minimize shrinkage, and let the sheets air dry afterward. A third alternative, if you just can't wait, is to place each pressed sheet between blotters and iron them dry.

Once the sheets of handmade paper are dry, they can be stacked and put under some books or boards for several days to flatten them. Sheets can then be used in card-making.

Note: To make highly textured sheets like Leslie Ebert's (opposite), you can couch on a textured surface or deliberately wrinkled piece of fabric, press out some of the water with a sponge, and air dry.

MAKING ENVELOPES

It's easy to make a handmade paper envelope with deckle edges by purchasing a plastic insert to fit your papermaking mold and holding it in place as you scoop up pulp from the vat. These are readily available in various sizes and shapes from papermaking suppliers. You can also make your own insert by steaming and opening out an envelope, tracing it on a piece of waterproofed foam board trimmed to fit your mold, and then cutting an envelope shaped hole in the center of the foam board to collect the pulp.

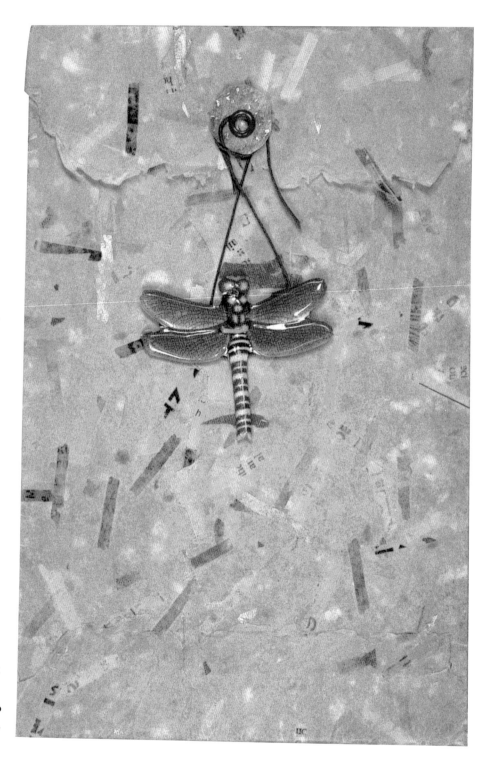

A deckle-edged handmade paper envelope by Claudia K. Lee. A paper button and tin dragonfly ornament playfully decorate the design, which is reminiscent of the old-style manila business envelopes.

Suminagashi Marbling

Suminagashi marbled designs are made by floating rings of color on water, blowing or fanning the rings into meandering or jagged lines, and applying an absorbent paper to make a contact print. This technique was practiced in the tenth century as a way of creating backgrounds for calligraphic art. It is being rediscovered in this century as a way to create beautiful papers to use in paper art and card design. This is the simplest type of marbling, and can be enjoyed by children as well as adults.

What You'll Need

Marbling tray. A photo tray or kitty litter pan will be fine for learning suminagashi. Later, you may want buy a professional marbling tray with a separate rinse and skim section to make it easier to rinse your marbled papers and skim off excess color from the water in your tray.

Rinse board and bucket. A purchased marbling tray will include a rinse board. If you're using a makeshift tray, you'll need a cookie sheet and a nearby sink or bucket to rinse papers that require removal of excess color.

Water jug. For dispensing the rinse water.

Drying rack or lines. A clothesline strung with PVC pipe is the ideal drying equipment to hold wet suminagashi papers.

Color containers. A small plastic watercolor mixing tray with six

This card was created by layering multiple-image suminagashi paper panels and foliage.

divided sections can be used to hold the Japanese dyes. An ice cube tray can be used as a substitute.

Eyedroppers. These are used to transfer color and Photo-Flo dispersant into the color containers.

Brushes. Inexpensive bamboo brushes that taper to a point, like Series BB by Loew-Cornell, are excellent for suminagashi. A #3 or #4 brush is fine. You'll need at least three of them.

Brush rest. This is not essential, but a small plastic brush rest will come in handy.

Paper towels. These are useful for drawing excess water out of your brushes.

Newspaper strips. Newspaper cut in 2"-wide strips are used to skim off dust before printing and skim off excess color remaining between prints.

Colors. Begin suminagashi marbling using Boku Undo marbling dyes. After you've gained some experience with these coloring agents, you may want to experiment with Japanese ink sticks or cake colors to produce your own Japanese inks.

Kodak Photo-Flo 200. This photographic chemical, a substitute for the pine resin traditionally used in Japan, helps disperse the Boku Undo colors, enabling them to spread and float. When added

to a teaspoon of water, the solution creates a clear liquid used to preserve open areas between rings of color.

Paper. Absorbent papers work best for Suminagashi marbling. Japanese papers such as kozo, Moriki, and Okawara as well as many handmade, block print, and charcoal papers marble well, as does Loew-Cornell's Oriental Rice paper. Other papers with a high cotton content sometimes also work. Experiment to find your favorite.

PREPARING TO MARBLE

Fill your marbling tray with water to a depth of about 1½". Place a teaspoon of two different Boku Undo colors in two sections of your divided color container. Place a teaspoon of water in another section. Add a single drop of Photo-Flo to each color and to the teaspoon of water and

stir it in well. Skim off any dust that may have settled on the water by dragging a newspaper strip down the length of the tray.

APPLYING AND PATTERNING THE COLORS

Using a different brush for each color, stir the colors again and in the center of the marbling tray, touch the surface of the water with the tip of one color-filled brush, releasing a circle of color. Now touch this circle of color with the tip of the brush containing the stirred clear solution to push the color into a ring. Alternately apply color and clear dispersing solution until a number of concentric rings are formed. Then gently blow the rings into a design. Most people start out by holding a single brush

---

To skim off dust or excess color between prints, hold a newspaper strip as shown and drag it down the length of the marbling tray.

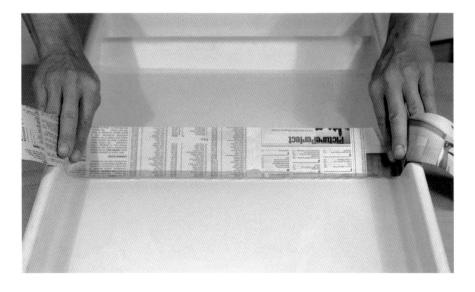

 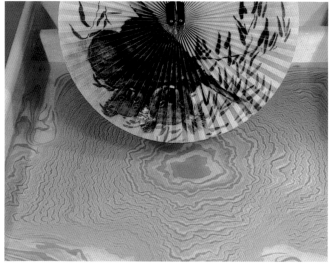

 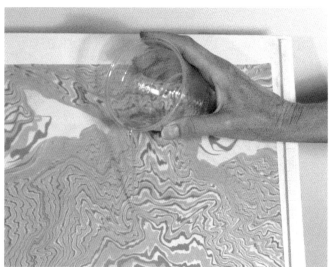

Top row, left: With a little practice you can easily hold three brushes to alternately apply color and dispersant and build up a number of concentric rings. Top row, right: Fanning the floating rings into a pattern of jagged lines.

Bottom row, left: To print your design, lay a sheet of absorbent paper onto the floating colors. Steady one hand on the far corner of the tray and ease the far edge of the paper onto the water. Hold that edge securely while you lower the rest of the sheet, until the entire paper is down. Bottom row, right: Rinsing the printed paper to remove any excess color.

in each hand, but quickly graduate to holding two color brushes in one hand, as shown above, to deposit color more quickly and keep a rhythm going.

When you've gained some practice, try working with several colors. Create concentric rings by alternating color with the clear solution or applying one color atop another without a clear ring. Deposit color in various sections of the tray, building up several rings before moving to a new location.

Suminagashi patterns often fea-ture meandering lines of color made by blowing gently from the side of the tray, or jagged lines of color made by blowing sharply down from overhead. A hand-held fan can also be used to create jagged lines. If you marble with very little water in your tray, you can create unusual designs by dragging a single hair through the color rings. I've devised a special tool that also works to produce the same image, by taping a cat whisker (volunteered by my cat, Camille) to the wrong end of a bamboo brush.

MAKING THE PRINT

After patterning, slowly lay a sheet of absorbent paper on top of the floating image, being careful not to slide it or flop it down and disturb the design. If you're working with a very fragile paper, leave 1" of the paper dry to help you pick it up.

RINSING, DRYING, AND FLATTENING THE SHEET

If you see colors bleeding, lay your paper on the rinse board and rinse by pouring water gently over it. Then drape it over a drying rack or clothesline. When the paper is dry, you can place it under a board to flatten it or iron it on the unmarbled side.

MARBLING ENVELOPES

You can, of course, create envelopes from your suminagashi papers, but you can also marble purchased envelopes to complement your cards. Most envelopes I've tried accept and retain the colors well although the images tend to be a bit more pale, but this makes it easier to letter over when addressing them. You can also use frisket film or iron on freezer paper to block out and preserve an addressing area on the front of the envelope before marbling it.

A word of caution: When you lay your marbled envelopes out to dry, be careful that the flaps are open so they don't seal themselves!

OVERMARBLING

To create a double-image design, marble a dry sheet a second time. The intersecting lines will create new patterns and colors, producing tighter and more complicated looking images.

Note: More complex types of marbling—oil color marbling and watercolor marbling—are also perfect for producing papers to be used on cards and envelopes. Although the scope of this book

How to hold two suminagashi brushes in one hand. The wide spaces between rings of color in this double-image suminagashi background paper were made by allowing more clear dispersant solution to flow from the brush before using the color brush again.

doesn't permit covering all types of marbling, complete in-depth instructions can be found in my book *The Ultimate Marbling Handbook* published by Watson-Guptill Publications.

Chalk Marbling

Chalk marbling is a kind of faux marbling—very simple to do, but quite effective for producing colorful papers to be used individually or layered to create a lively greeting card or invitation. Paula Beardell Krieg sent me some charming cards with chalk marbled panels on the front that needed no further embellishment (below). She also sent the following instructions for creating vivid papers like those pictured.

What You'll Need

Paper. Most medium-weight drawing papers will do. Paula usually uses Arches Text Laid.

Chalk. The softer, and more brightly colored, the better. Paula uses them all, but gets the best results using Freart Colored Paper Chalk, by Prang.

Rectangular tray. A lasagna pan is a good example. It should be larger than your piece of paper; she usually uses the 9" x 13" size.

Tap water.

Waxed paper.

Hot iron.

Plastic serrated knife.

Clean scrap paper.

Chalk-marbled cards by Paula Beardell Krieg.

Technique

Fill the tray to about 1" from the top. Using the knife, scrape the chalk into the tray. The chalk will float. Add as many colors as you like, but work somewhat quickly, as the chalk will sink after awhile. Lay the paper on the chalk-covered surface of the water, lift it off after about a second, and set it aside. Allow the paper to dry completely. After the papers are completely dry, lay the paper, chalk-side-up, on scrap paper. Cover the chalked image with a piece of waxed paper. Lay scrap paper on the waxed paper (this is to protect your iron). With a hot iron, iron the layers so that the wax transfers to the chalked paper, thus sealing it.

$\mathcal{B}$ubble Marbling

The technique for another type of faux marbling, bubble marbling, was also provided by Paula Kreig. Unlike the many pastel bubble-marbled papers I have seen, Paula's have a more intense coloring that most people find difficult to achieve. Paula's secrets follow.

What You'll Need

Paper. For the most saturated color, sized paper, such as watercolor paper, or coated paper work the best. Just about any paper can be used for pastel designs.

Several 12-oz. bowls. You'll need one for each bubble color. Paula generally uses Styrofoam bowls, for easy cleanup, or plastic bowls that come with lids that seal well in case she wants to save the solution for next time.

Color. Paula has used cheap powdered tempera, acrylic paints, and handmade paper pigments. All have their own charms. The important thing to keep in mind is to use intensely colored paints. The amount you use will be determined by how rich or muted you want your colors to be. She has gotten good results by stirring 2 tablespoons of Liquitex acrylic paint into 6 oz. of water that had

3 tablespoons of soap in it. Definitely stay away from watercolor inks, as they are too dilute.

Dawn Ultra dishwashing soap. Others may work—this is a favorite.

Tap water.

Drinking straws.

Spoons for mixing color.

Technique

Prepare one bowl of soapy water for each color you intend to use. Add about 3 tablespoons of soap to about 6 oz. of water. Add color. The amount of paint you use will be determined by the kind of paint you are using, and how intense you want the color to be.

A bubble-marbled card by Paula Beardell Krieg.

Blend the mixture well, then use your straw to blow bubbles into the mixture (like you used to blow bubbles into milk as a child). Lightly lay some scrap paper on the bubbles, check the image, and add more color if needed.

When your colors are satisfactory, blow fresh bubbles. Then lay your good paper lightly onto the bubbles, and the image will instantly transfer onto the paper. Move on to the next color as desired until your paper is sufficiently covered. Blow fresh bubbles prior to laying the paper down each time—bubbles that are even 20 seconds old will not transfer color well.

Paste Paper Designs

To create a paste paper you simply dampen a sheet of paper, coat it with colored paste, and draw various implements through the paste to displace it and create patterns. Paste paper designs have been used to decorate book covers and endpapers for centuries. They're now escaping the library shelves to be used in card design as well as other paper arts. With this type of paper decorating it's easy to make a wide range of colorful graphic designs to use as decorative panels for card fronts, to layer with other background papers behind a central motif, or to collage with other papers for a great greeting, announcement, or invitation.

Lea Everse stamped and layered my gold and silver paste-painted papers to create this charming tasseled card. Square stamp image by Magenta.

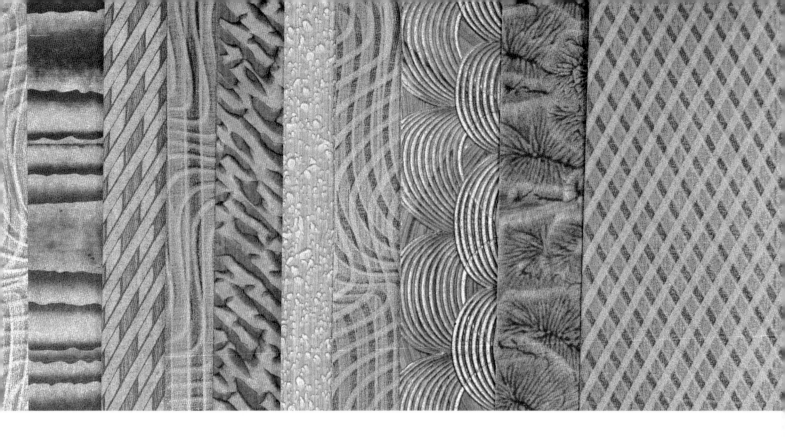

What You'll Need

Cooking pot. A 2-quart saucepan will be fine for cooking up the paste. A microwavable bowl can be used instead for microwaved paste.

Measuring cup.

Teaspoons. These can be old garage sale items. They are used for stirring the paint into the prepared paste.

Sponges. These are used for wetting the paper, for making sponge prints in paste, if desired, and for cleanup.

Gloves (optional).

Small plastic water bucket. This gives you a place to dip the sponge for cleanup and for sponging down the paper to be pasted.

Brushes. Several large 2" to 4" high quality house painting brushes are needed, one for each color. Don't purchase inexpensive ones—they lose their bristles in the middle of making designs!

Paste containers. Plastic food storage containers with snap-tight lids are ideal. They need to be big enough to accommodate your paintbrush.

Work surface. A piece of Plexiglas 3" bigger all around than the paper you plan to pattern is a good investment. Alternatives include an old formica or enamel tabletop.

Large shallow tub. A large plastic storage box filled with water is perfect for wetting your papers.

Large, fine mesh strainer.

Stamped, combed, and roller-printed paste papers.

Patterning tools. Many household tools and found objects can be used to make paste papers. Plastic hair picks, rubber stamps, and chopsticks are but a few of the many patterning tools you may already have on hand. Other great implements for making designs include metal and rubber graining combs found in paint stores, crumpled pieces of newspaper, multiple-line calligraphy pens, and potters' tools. Rubber brayers carved with a mat knife can also yield interesting designs. Check your what-not drawer for other possibilities.

Paper. Most nonabsorbent medium-weight papers are fine for making paste paper designs.

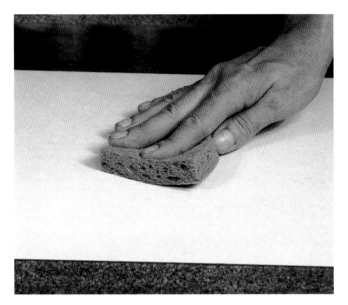

Above left: Sponging down the wet paper to flatten it and remove some of the moisture.

Above right: Brushing a layer of acrylic-colored paste on the dampened paper.

The paper must be strong enough to withstand having tools drawn across it in a dampened state without shredding. I use Canson Mi-Teintes, Strathmore, and Mohawk Superfine papers, but many offset printing papers also work great.

Paints. A good brand of acrylic paint, like Golden or Liquitex, gives excellent results. Don't buy fluid acrylics, as they tend to dilute the paste too much. Invest in a range of colors and be sure to include some metallics and pearlescent paints. You can also add some Pearlex or mica powders to acrylics to make them sparkle.

Paste. Rice flour, wheat flour, cornstarch, and methyl cellulose can all be used to make paste (or starch) papers.

MAKING THE PASTE

Many paste papermakers swear by a favorite recipe. The cornstarch recipe that I use when making papers for cards is very easy to make and produces a paper with a smooth finish.

Mix ¼ cup cornstarch with ¼ cup water until well blended. Then add 1 cup water and heat the mixture while stirring until it resembles a thick custard. Finally, stir in ½ cup water to thin it. Let the paste cool and thicken before pushing it through a strainer to remove any lumps and then dividing it into bowls to be colored.

Microwave recipe: After the water and cornstarch are blended and the cup of water has been added, instead of heating the starch mixture on the stove, try heating it in your microwave. Check it and stir at 1-minute intervals until it reaches the thickened stage. Depending upon the power of your microwave this can take as little as 2-3 minutes. Next, stir in the remaining water and let it cool.

COLORING THE PASTE

Start by adding 2 – 3 teaspoons of paint to ½ cup of paste. Adjust the amount of paint depending upon the color intensity desired; the color will dry on the paper a bit lighter than it looks in the container. If you want to darken a color a bit, add just a touch of black—it can easily overpower another color. Add some metallics or pearlescents to your colors to make the papers shimmer.

PREPARING THE PAPER

Relax your paper in a tray or sink of water by dragging the paper through the water, wetting both sides, and then letting it drip for a moment before carrying it over to the Plexiglas and laying it flat. Apply pressure as you stroke the paper from the center outward with a damp sponge to remove excess water, press out any air bubbles, and completely flatten it. If any wrinkles remain in the paper, your patterning will highlight them.

Applying the Paste

Fill a large 2"– 4" paintbrush with paste and brush it evenly on your paper. Use horizontal strokes to cover the paper with a thin layer of paste and then go back over the paper with vertical strokes to assure a good color application. If you're using different colored pastes on the same sheet, brush in one direction only to avoid totally mixing the colors and making them muddy. Instead, try letting the colored

pastes overlap slightly to make subtle color blends.

Patterning Principles

Allover tightly grouped repeat patterns are easy to make and are of an appropriate size for card design. Explore them by making a row of diagonal or horizontal lines with a pick or comb and then crossing them at regular intervals with vertical ones. Use a calligraphy pen to make a wavy line next to a straight one. When using combs, try angling the combing tool slightly toward you as you draw it through the paste. It will help to make the movements smoother and the designs more pronounced.

Vary the direction and type of movement you make to create

rigid straight lines, eccentric zig-zags, or long gentle curves or scallops. It's easy to create designs that not only decorate paper to be used on cards created for stationery, but also relate to the themes of your greeting or congratulatory cards and the stamped or stenciled art you might place atop the paste papers. A gentle waved paste design might be used as a mountainous background for a card bearing a stamped bicycle to congratulate someone for a recent win in a bike race. A scalloped design might depict waves on a card embossed with a boat to say, "Happy Summer."

_____

Using a rubber graining comb to create a scallop design in the paste. Successive layers of scallops will create a tight design suitable for card use.

Explore making prints in paste by stamping a paste-covered paper with various objects. A crumpled piece of plastic wrap or newspaper, rubber stamps, and carved linoleum blocks can be used. Objects made of rubber, cork, metal, wood, and plastic will all displace paste if you use them to strike the coated paper. To get the best image, wipe off the paste that clings to them before stamping a second time. Two pasted sheets of paper can be

pressed together face to face and then pulled apart to create a textured print resembling foliage. Just pressing your hand into the paste can also yield a great mossy design. Do this sparingly, however, as some of the paints may not be safe for repeated skin contact.

Finishing

Dry paste papers by draping them over a rack or line covered with PVC pipe so they don't dry with a crimp in them. (If they do, you can iron them on their reverse sides.)

Be sure to use a wet sponge to wipe off any paste that's left on your work surface before beginning another sheet.

Creating Multiple-image Designs

After a sheet has dried, you can re-wet it and coat it with paste again to create a second image on top of the first. The colors and pattern of the primary image will peek through and can produce a sheet with a lot of dimension. Combed papers take on quite a brilliance if they're coated with gold or silver paste and patterned a second time. Rubber and plastic tools are safest to use when making combed multiple-image designs. Redampened paste can be a bit fragile, and metal combs may abrade initial images.

A card created by Lea Everse using some of my tightly combed double-image papers. Metallic-gold-colored paste was used as a second coat on the papers. "Joy" stamp by Rubberstiltken. Holly stamp by Co-Motion.

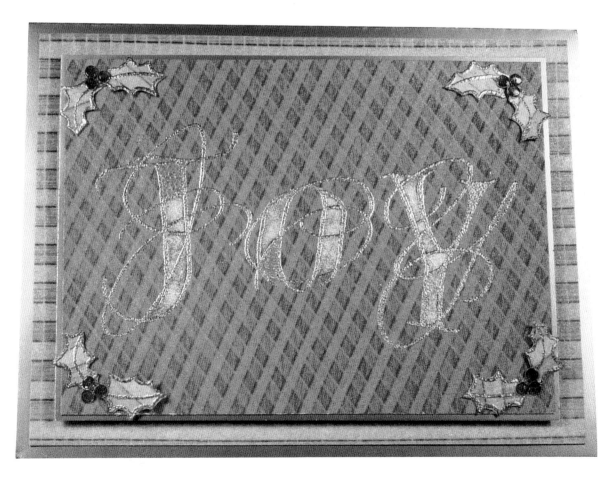

ℬatik

ℬatik or wax-resist papers are easy to make and can be used to create a background paper for a photo or produce an exotic-looking paper to grace your folded card stock. Although usually done on text-weight drawing paper, using watercolor paints, or dyes, Hélène Métivier creates gorgeous batik papers by painting sturdy rice papers with fabric dyes and wax.

The principle behind the batik process is as follows. When wax is applied to a material (fabric or paper), it forms a barrier that repels any liquid color applied over it. If you start out with a white sheet of paper, for instance, drip spots of wax on it, and then coat the paper with a wash of blue dye, you'll wind up with a blue sheet of paper with white spots. If you then dip a brush in wax and make random brush strokes on the paper, followed by a wash of green dye, you'll have a green sheet of paper with white spots protected by the first waxing and blue brush strokes where the second application of wax preserved the blue paint.

What You'll Need

Wax. Begin with a mixture of paraffin and beeswax or batik wax, purchased from an art supply store.

A card featuring batik paper panels by Hélène Métivier.

Double boiler. This is the safest way to melt the wax.

Wax applicator. Large and small disposable watercolor brushes can be used to brush and splatter on the wax.

Paper. Many types of paper can be used, as long as they can withstand being wet with liquid colors. Some of the softer papers may retain more of the wax, but it shouldn't pose a problem.

Colors. Rather transparent colors like liquid dyes, inks, and inexpensive watercolors can be used.

Color applicators. Wide bamboo, polyfoam, and mop brushes will deliver a good wash of color. (I like to use a 1" oval mop from Loew-Cornell.)

Newspapers. You'll need plenty of newspapers to protect tabletops from wax and color and to absorb wax as it's ironed out of papers.

Iron. You'll need an iron to remove the wax from papers after you've applied your last coat of dye. Use one without steam vents if possible, as wax can block the vents.

TECHNIQUE

Although fine line tjanting tools can be used to make traditional batik designs, it's great fun to make abstract designs by brushing, splashing, and splattering the wax on. Metal tools like a potato masher can also be dipped in wax and applied to the papers.

Begin by melting some of your wax in a double boiler, being careful not to let it overheat. It can give off noxious smoke or actually ignite if it gets too hot! When the wax has melted, dip your inexpensive brush in the wax and begin making designs on a light sheet of paper. Work quickly—the wax will begin to dry almost immediately.

When the wax is dry, apply a light value color wash over the entire sheet of paper. Let the color dry and then brush, drip, or splatter on more wax, followed by another wash of a darker harmonious color. Build up layers of wax and color, bearing in mind that each coat of wax will maintain the last color applied. (Don't be concerned if your paper looks

Adding another layer of wax to a dye-batiked paper by Hélène Métivier.

less than beautiful at this point.) When the final coat of color has dried, it's time to unveil your masterpiece by removing the wax from the sheet. To do this, sandwich the paper batik between several layers of newspaper and press it with a warm iron. Keep changing the newspaper and ironing until the wax has been ironed out of the sheet.

Crayon Batik

Traditional batik done on fabric often contains a cracked background, which occurs naturally when the batik, especially fabrics heavily waxed with paraffin, are immersed in a dye bath. Crayon batik mimics this feature on paper in a much simpler way. Paula Beardell Kreig contributed stunning cards (right) and shared her version of this neat batik technique.

What You'll Need

Paper. Any medium-weight drawing paper will do. Paula favors Arches Text Laid.

Crayons. Use Crayolas. Buy the big box and try glitter crayons, too.

Acrylic paint.

Acrylic medium (optional). If necessary, this can be used to thin the paint so that it brushes on smoothly.

Sponge.

Paintbrush. Select one 2" wide, to use with the acrylic paint.

Clean scrap paper.

Iron. Set it to medium hot.

Water.

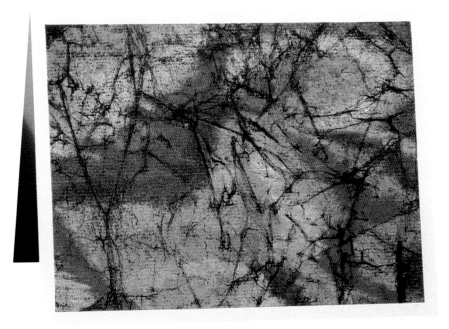

Crayon batik cards by Paula Beardell Krieg that mimic the cracked background often found on batik fabrics.

TECHNIQUE

Crayon heavily onto the paper; be sure to cover every inch. When you are done coloring, crumple the paper up into a tight ball. This creates cracks in the crayon wax, which will eventually give the paper the batik effect. Open the paper and smooth it out flat.

Make sure your iron is on and set to a medium heat, then completely cover the crayoned surface with a generous wash of black acrylic paint. You need to work quickly, as you do not want the acrylic paint to start drying. Next, use a wet sponge to remove the paint. The acrylic color will be left behind in the cracks.

Now, sandwich your paper crayoned-side-down between two layers of clean scrap paper. Iron the sandwich until your crayon-batiked paper is dry. The crayon will melt and create a stunning card-decorating paper with a smooth surface and cracked background.

Paula's heavily crayoned papers, shown crumpled to create cracks in preparation for the black acrylic wash (left) and showing the batik effect after the black wash is removed (right).

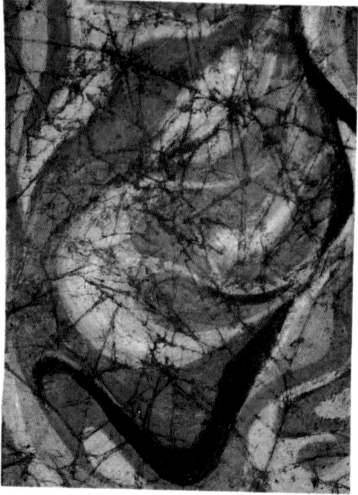

Rubber-stamped Batik Cards

Another type of batik paper can be created by using rubber stamps and clear embossing powder to produce thermal-embossed resists instead of wax. Vonda Jones began her card (below) by coating her rubber stamp petrograph designs with a clear embossing ink and stamping them on white mulberry paper. Next she applied clear embossing powder and thermally embossed the designs (see Chapter 2, page 40).

Vonda next chose three different colored Marvy Matchable Dye Ink Pads and stroked them onto the embossed paper in a direct-to-paper technique for applying color. This allowed the resisted image to appear. Vonda often does additional stamping with the same dye inks and the stamp used as the resist image to further decorate a batik paper destined for use on her delightful cards.

A rubber-stamped batik card by Vonda Jones. Stamp design by Copper Leaf Creations.

$\mathcal{C}$ special techniques for
REATING
CARDS
with texture and dimension

There are many special card-making techniques that can give your card extra dimension. Some of the techniques, like paper casting, paper rolling, quilling, and tile designs, will give your card so much dimension or make them appear so fragile that you may think it's impossible to send them through the mail. Very few of the techniques that follow will prevent you from sending your cards, although you may want to use a padded or rigid envelope or cover them with a thin sheet of foam to be extra safe. Additional postage and the words "hand stamp" may have to be placed on the envelopes as well. Dimensional cards, whether they are delivered in person or sent to the recipient, will be among those most appreciated and most likely to be framed and hung on the wall.

A dimensional cast-paper card made with colored pulp by Barbara Fletcher.

Dimensional Cast-paper Cards

The same pulp you used to create sheets of paper for card-making can be used to create cast-paper ornamentation to be used in card design. Uncolored wet pulp can be pressed into a purchased plastic mold to create an ornament like the butterfly pictured below, or found molds such as muffin tins or candy molds can be used to give shape to colored paper castings. Oregon artist Leslie Ebert creates sensational cast paper by handcarving soft printers' block with linoleum-cutting tools as though she was creating a rubber stamp. Leslie then uses the carving and the block on which it is made as a surface on which to couch the extra thick pulp she lifts from the papermaking vat. Using a sponge, Leslie presses the thick sheet of paper pulp into the depressions in her carved block and presses out as much water as possible. She allows the paper to completely dry before removing it from the mold and airbrushing it with transparent pigments. Although Leslie creates her own paper pulp, she notes that card artists who want to skip the pulping steps can also purchase ready-made pulp from a papermaking supplier. Leslie also suggests that airbrushing effects can be approximated by applying two or three related colors of spray paint to your casting in broad strokes, finishing with just a hint of gold paint to accentuate the surface of the work.

A card by Brenda Volpe featuring a cast-paper butterfly made with a plastic mold by Arnold Grummer. Embossed and colored paper by K & Co.

Above: An air-brushed cast-paper card by Leslie Ebert and the carved mold from which it was made on the right.

Left: Leslie carving a linoleum block to be used on another cast-paper work.

Below: Leslie using an airbrush to begin layering colors on an uncolored cast-paper card.

to cure. At this point, she can begin placing her colored pulps in the mold to create the cast paper. She often adds brightly colored recycled papers to the cotton and abaca fibers when preparing the pulp.

Barbara notes that because these papers already have binders in them, she doesn't need to add anything to strengthen the pulp. A mold release is not necessary either, as the pulp shrinks as it dries and releases itself from the plaster cast quite easily. Like Leslie, Barbara often airbrushes her castings with fabric dyes to intensify the colors before adhering the cast paper to folded card stock.

Above left: An assortment of humorous dimensional cast-paper cards by Barbara Fletcher.

Below left: Barbara among the colorful pulp-filled buckets in her papermaking studio. She is pictured pressing wet pulp into one of her cardmaking molds. Below right: After the pulp is dry, Barbara can easily lift her card front from the mold.

Massachusetts artist Barbara Fletcher creates even more dimensional paper castings by first creating a form in nonhardening sculptor's clay. Next she covers the clay with hydrocal plaster. After the plaster sets, Barbara removes the clay and waits about 24 hours for the plaster

$\mathcal{Q}$uilled Cards

Quilling or paper filigree has been practiced since Victorian times to create beautiful and romantic greeting cards. By rolling narrow strips of paper into coiled shapes and gluing them together to form intricate designs, you can create the perfect decoration for a love note. Floral designs are most often made with quilled shapes, but snowflakes can also be crafted easily to decorate a card announcing a winter party or to invite someone on a skiing excursion. The quilling can cover the entire front of your card or be placed off to the side with ribbon embellishments to allow for a written or stamped greeting.

A snowflake quilled card by Mary Anne Landfield.

Quilling paper. Packs of pre-cut quilling paper approximately 24" long and ⅛" – ¼" wide are sold in craft and art supply shops. They're available in an array of colors and are inexpensive.

Quilling tool. Paper can be coiled around many types of implements, including rounded

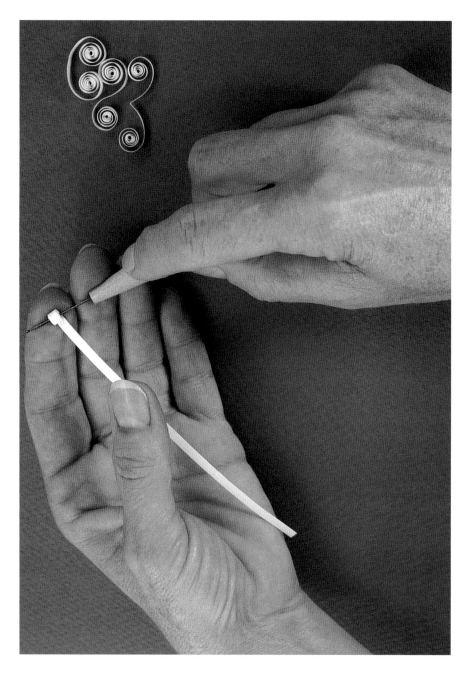

Using a quilling tool to roll a coil.

Scissors. These are used to cut strips for open coils, where both ends of the shape will be exposed. Strips used for closed shapes should be torn, rather than cut, to make their ends less visible.

Glue. White glue, like Sobo, or a glue pen will hold closed coils in place, join quilled pieces, and attach quilled designs to their backings.

Glue applicator. A toothpick can be used to apply tiny spots of glue to quilled shapes.

Tweezers. These are helpful for placing tiny quilled pieces inside open quilled designs.

Waxed paper. Working over waxed paper when applying glue to close a coil or assemble quilled shapes will prevent designs from sticking to your working surface.

Optional equipment.
Washers. Metal or rubber washers with various diameters make good jigs that assure that coils expand to the same size before they're glued.

Quilling board and straight pins. A piece of foamcore covered with a sheet of graph paper will allow you to create a quilling board with a grid for lining up and measuring quilled pieces. Cover the quilling board with a piece of waxed paper to prevent glued pieces from sticking to it. Use straight pins to hold designs in place before gluing them together.

toothpicks, large needles, hat pins, and even bird feather quills (thought to be the original paper support). A more narrow tool, of course, will produce a coil with a smaller diameter center. If you have difficulty creating consistent shapes with a makeshift tool, you may find that investing in a purchased tool with a narrow shank and substantial handle makes rolling paper easier. Avoid tools with a paper slot in one end. They speed up the quilling process, but, unfortunately, leave a crease in the center of each quilled shape.

TECHNIQUE

Quilled designs are comprised of coils which can be either closed or open. The closed coil is secured by having the outside end glued down. In an open coil, sometimes called a scroll, the end remains unglued and the coil can relax and expand.

Rolling a closed coil. To begin rolling a closed coil, tear off a 4" strip of quilling paper. Holding your tool as shown (opposite), wind the torn end of the strip behind and around the quilling tool. Use your thumb and forefinger to begin rolling the strip into a coil. Try to apply even pressure and guide each round of paper so that it sits on top of the previous one. Continue quilling until you've rolled the entire strip of paper, then remove the coil from your tool, let it expand slightly, and apply a dot of glue to the torn edge. Hold the glued edge in place for a moment to glue it down, closing the coil.

Rolling an open coil or scroll. An open coil or scroll is rolled exactly like a closed coil, except that you don't glue down the end. If both ends are to remain exposed in a quilled work, you'll want to cut, rather than tear the quilling paper.

Basic coil and scroll designs. The following directions apply to the snowflake card on page 89:

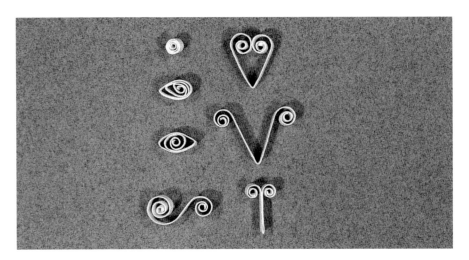

Peg. Roll a tight coil and glue the end down before removing it from the quilling tool.

Loose coil. Roll a coil loosely, remove it from the quilling tool, and let it expand some before gluing the end down.

Teardrop. Pinch one side of a loose coil.

Eye-shaped coil. Gently pinch both sides of a loose coil.

S-shaped scroll. Roll one half or a strip into the center, then flip the strip over and roll the other half.

Heart scroll. Crease the strip in the middle and roll a full scroll toward the "valley" side of the crease.

V-scroll. Crease the paper strip in the middle and roll a full scroll toward the "mountain side" of the crease.

V-scroll variation. Glue the sides of the V-scroll together to form a T.

The basic quilled designs that Mary Anne Landfield used in her card are the peg, teardrop, eye-shaped coil, S-shaped scroll, heart scroll, V-scroll, and a variation of the V-scroll.

CREATING AND ASSEMBLING A QUILLED CARD DESIGN

Some quillers like to make multiple filigree shapes and then move the pieces around until they find a pleasing way to decorate the front of a folded card. Others prefer to draw a pattern and make quilled pieces to fit. Regardless of which method you choose, be sure to work over waxed paper, so that when pieces are positioned, you can apply glue and assemble them.

If your design is complicated, place your pattern on a quilling board and pin each element in place before gluing. When the quilled design is dry, check to see that all joins are complete and then transfer the quillwork to a folded card. Apply tiny spots of glue to the back of the piece before lightly pressing it in place on your card front.

$\mathcal{U}$sing Pressed $\mathcal{F}$lowers and Foliage

$\mathcal{P}$ressed flowers and leaves add romance to a greeting card. You can press and dry flowers you have picked on a walk with your special friend or press a flower from a bouquet given to you as a gift and place it on a thank you card. You can purchase a flower press or use an old telephone directory. Simply sandwich flowers between ½"- thick layers of telephone directory pages and weight the top with a heavy board or stack of books until the flowers are dry. Many companies like

Nature's Pressed offer leaves and flowers that have been professionally pressed. They are available in a wide range of vivid colors.

To use purchased dried flowers or those you've dried yourself, simply brush white glue on them and press them in place on your folded card stock. Although these cards will be fine to give to a recipient in person, if you're mailing

them you may want to further protect them by brushing on a coat of thinned white glue that remains flexible and dries clear.

Another way to use flowers is to create botanical ribbon cards like the one pictured by Bren Riesinger (below). No need to worry about your flowers breaking or not laying flat with this technique. In order to make a ribbon card, dried flowers must be crumbled and sprinkled over a mesh ribbon that has been coated with glue or strips of double-sided adhesive. If you use glue, wait for the adhesive to dry before using more white glue to adhere the ribbon to your card front. Bren recommends you use a

botanical like hops for the final layer of crumbled flowers because they break up into a fine dust that will fill in any spaces left by larger crumbled flowers.

Skeleton leaves are another type of foliage that can be used to create handmade cards. They often appear in collages, and can be used in leaf printing, but sometimes become the singular focus of a card front. They're available in most scrapbooking and stamp stores today in a wide range of sizes and colors. Some are made of a synthetic material and others are made with actual leaves that have been bleached to remove their inner parts.

Opposite: Flowers were glued on and embedded in this handmade paper card to wish the recipient "Happy Spring."

Below: The botanical ribbon card by Bren Riesinger is composed of dried crumbled flowers.

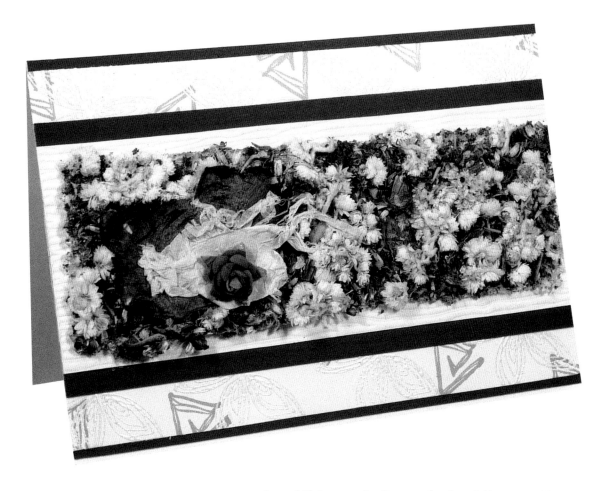

$\mathcal{U}$sing Metallic Flakes

Faux gilding, using metallic leafing flakes, will add elegance to any card you create. The flakes look like real gold, copper, and silver, and when placed on a sticky surface will add a brilliance that looks sensational. Several companies make these flakes and some recommend using a liquid adhesive, others a dry adhesive, on which to place the flakes. When the adhesive is tacky you press the flakes in place and brush off the excess with a soft brush.

Lea Everse created these cards by applying small amounts of gilding adhesive to select areas of a skeleton leaf and then laying the leafing flakes in place. Another way to use the flakes is to purchase a leafing pen, which allows you to write with a glue that will accept the flakes. Lea Everse experi-

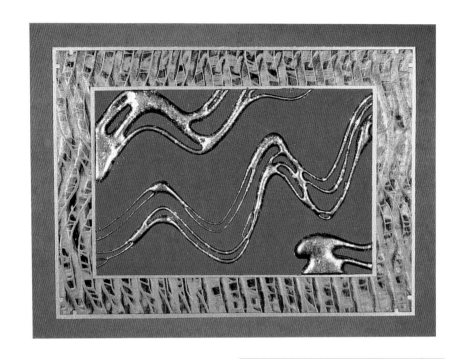

mented by applying the leafing flakes to an image created with hot glue with the wonderful results pictured above. The leafing adhered perfectly even though the hot glue was dry and cooled.

Above: To create this card, Lea Everse experimented by applying leafing flakes to hot glue.

Below: Here, Lea layered a skeleton leaf gilded with metallic flakes over one of my paste papers and other pieces of card stock.

Creating Tile or Quilt Designs

Tile or quilt designs are another easy way to create a card with lots of dimension. The tiles can be made from mat board squares or triangles, or layered paper cut into square or diamond shapes. Often, this type of card utilizes a rubber-stamped image or photo that is cut into squares and mounted on mat board and then rearranged so that the image is not recognizable. At other times a rubber-stamped image may be repeated on different colored squares of mat board as with Hélène Métivier's card (below right).

I used foreign postage stamps, mounting them with dry adhesive on photocopies of calendar pages to begin the card pictured (below left). Then, using dry adhesive, I mounted two different layers of mat board together as a colorful base for each of the stamp and calendar page images. Each four-layered square was then placed on two layers of card stock and mounted on the front of the card. The graduated size of the elements comprising each finished square helps give the card extra dimension.

When creating tile designs it is important to measure and create guide lines lightly in pencil so that your squares line up. Eyeballing the distances between squares horizontally as well as vertically is very difficult and precision is important to the success of this type of card.

Below left: Recycled papers like these foreign postage stamps and old calendar pages can be used to make decorative tile designs.

Below right: Hélène Métivier of Magenta Rubber Stamps stamped and cut squares of mat board to create this tile card.

Woven Card Designs

Weaving is another way to add interest to cards and envelopes. The weaving can be a simple tabby over, under pattern made by weaving horizontal weft strips through vertical warp slits you've made in your card stock, or a simple woven design can be made separately and then adhered to the card or envelope. Create different weaving patterns like those shown in the cards and envelope by Patti Quinn Hill by departing from the tabby weave and going over two or more

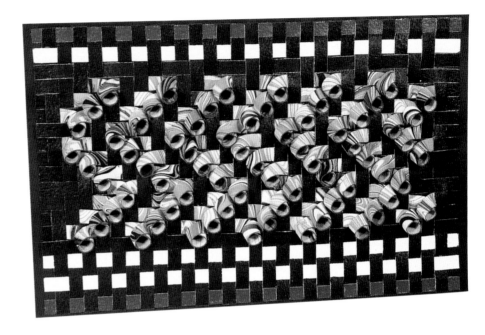

warp strips at a time (above). Woven cards with lots of dimension can be made by creating loops with your weft strips before weaving under the next available warp. Patti uses a pasta machine to cut ¼" weaving strips from heavy paper, but a paper cutter or X-acto knife and metal ruler can also be used.

Above: By creating loops in her weaving strips, Patti created an elaborate card with texture and dimension.

Below: A simple tabby-woven ornament can dress up cards and envelopes as shown in these works by Patty Quinn Hill.

$\mathscr{B}$argello Designs

$\mathscr{B}$argello designs, although they resemble weaving, are not true weaving because strips are adhered in place, not woven. Hélène Métivier, whose work is shown elsewhere in this book, is credited with adapting Bargello, a pattern often used by fabric quilters, to create paper quilts. Lea Everse created the Bargello card shown (right), using some of my paste papers.

What You'll Need

Paper. You'll need approximately 10 to 12 strips, ¼" wide by 6" long. These should be different colors or types of decorative paper.

Double-sided adhesive film.

Bone folder.

Sheet of text-weight paper.

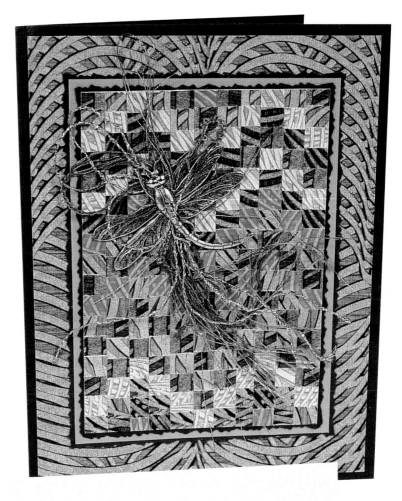

Above: A paste-paper Bargello design card by Lea Everse.

Below: Instead of being used in a Bargello design, the cut strips can also be used to form a decorative border as in this suminagashi marbled card by Jennifer Philippoff.

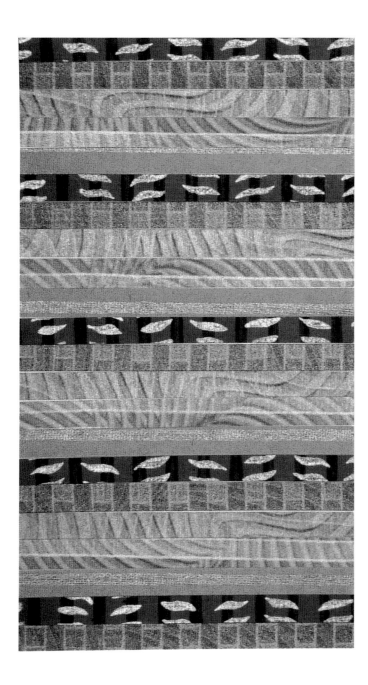

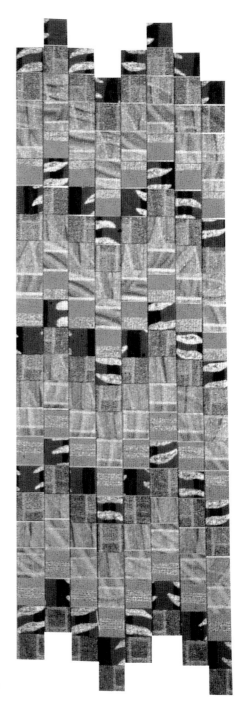

CREATING THE BARGELLO PANEL

Arrange the ¼" strips of paper on a piece of double-sided adhesive film, side by side (horizontally) lining them up as straight as possible and making sure that they butt up against each other. Burnish the strips with a bone folder so they adhere well. Next cut this block of strips into ¼" strips (vertically) so you wind up with strips of little colored squares. Remove the backing paper from these strips and place them onto a sheet of text-weight paper, arranging them to form a pattern by moving strips up or down a colored square to form a consistent pattern. When

Cutting and aligning the strips to form a Bargello design.

all strips are in place, trim the edges of the design to form a square or rectangular panel and layer it with other papers on your folded card.

Creating Collage Designs

Measuring won't be necessary for creating collage cards. This is a place to really exercise freedom of design—within reason. If you've never done collage before, it might be good to show a little restraint by beginning with a monochromatic color scheme or by limiting yourself to a few colors. Collage cards can look overdone if too many elements and colors are introduced without some unifying theme. Refer to the design principles mentioned in Chapter 1 for some guidance, then begin a treasure hunt for some papers, beads, bits of fabric, wire, feathers, or whatever else you'd like to use on your card. Just be sure that the elements you choose aren't too heavy for the card stock or other backing paper you use.

The repetition of shapes and colors in this mixed media Valentine's Day card with envelope by Betsy Veness creates an exciting, yet unified design.

I sometimes cut a piece of watercolor paper or card stock slightly smaller than the folded card I will mount it on and add collage materials to this backing paper. Creating a paper collage is easy. If you've saved brochures or menus from a trip you took, these can be combined with parts of the road map you followed, the photos you took, or the postcards you bought. Photocopies can be used instead of actual memorabilia.

Decorative papers you've created or purchased, of course, can also be used in a card collage along with found papers, such as old sheet music, report cards, wall paper, paint chip samples, etc.

Above left: The flash of gold mylar and rolled tubes of paper give Shirley Siegenthaler's collage dimension and focal points.

Left and below: Roxann Hutchinson created a complex found-paper collage (left) and had it reduced and photocopied to create greeting cards.

CREATING A DESIGN

You can cut or tear the paper into interesting shapes. Hold the paper and tear toward you to expose part of the paper's core or away from you to give it a clean but ragged edge. Use colored pencils or markers to decorate some of the paper's edges and repeat a color scheme or add a flash of bright color to add excitement to the work. Roll or crumple some of the papers to give them added dimension. Move the papers around and slip part of one behind another to overlap them. Check to see how papers look in a horizontal instead of vertical direction and "break the frame" by letting some of the papers extend beyond the edges of the backing paper so that they spill onto the folded card front.

Collage is a broad term and there are no hard and fast rules for assembling materials. Your collage can be an abstract, decorative, or representational work tied to a holiday, to remind your recipient of a shared experience, or to celebrate a particular success in her or his life. Let your intuition guide you as you move papers around without gluing them in place. Examine your successful and unsuccessful placements to get a feeling for what seems to work and what doesn't. You can create simple collage cards to give or construct elaborate works like Roxann Hutchison's collage and have them photocopied and reduced to produce multiple cards (opposite below). Collage

borders, like that by Jennifer Philippoff (above), can be made to leave an area on a card or envelope free for a calligraphed or stamped message or address.

ADHERING ELEMENTS IN PLACE

When you have an arrangement you like, begin to adhere the elements of your collage card in place. Follow the techniques for layering papers mentioned in Chapter 1. Using a dry adhesive will prevent the necessity of press-

An intricate collaged border design by Jennifer Philippoff that can be used on a card or envelope, leaving an area free for a stamped or handwritten greeting.

ing the paper overnight. When you begin to add heavier or dimensional elements, like wire or other found objects, however, you'll need to use glue appropriate for the type of material you wish to adhere in place. Stitching is another way to fasten collage materials to each other or to add a decorative accent to a collage card.

Cards Bearing Surprise Embellishments

A number of natural and manmade objects can be incorporated into your card design by placing them on top of a layered but not necessarily collaged card to make your greeting outstanding. Small toys, beads, charms, and other trinkets and surprises can be used to decorate the front of your handmade card instead of just being tucked inside it.

Hard candy and even a tiny chocolate bar can be glued to the front of a card intended to be hand delivered to someone who is "Sweet 16." A key can be a appropriate adornment for a card celebrating someone's first home purchase. A puzzle piece can be glued atop a card that says, "I'm puzzled, why haven't you written?" A dog biscuit surrounded by rubber-stamped images of paw prints would be a great card for a new puppy owner.

A scatter pin made out of papers that coordinate with your card design makes a fine greeting and gift that will surprise and delight the recipient. Just punch two holes to accept the pin through all background papers. Attached bookmarks that the recipient removes by tearing along a perforated line created with a tracing wheel or a Fiskars rolling trimmer with a perforating attachment is especially charming. If making a vertical format card, just make the back of the card about 1" wider than the front and decorate the bookmark with stamping, stenciling, or other embellishment. Add decorative ribbons to the top of the bookmark, if desired.

Above: Lea Everse attached a bookmark to her calligraphed "Get Well" card by slipping its corners beneath slits created in the background paper. Stamp design by Modern Illuminator.

Right: A magnet gift card by Lea Everse. Lea rubber stamped and colored in the image of the Japanese woman and adhered it to a piece of magnetic-backed vinyl. She hid a thin piece of sheet metal beneath the stamped central panel of her card on which the magnet is placed. A domino bead, Japan cord, and Chiyogami decorative paper complete the Oriental design.

Opposite: A key forms a prominent embellishment for this card featuring torn paper collaged, stamped, and thermal embossed squares by Brenda Volpe.

Postcards or bookmarks can be attached to a card front piggy-back style and slipped through slits made in the card stock or held in place with decorative photo corners. (This is one sure way of getting a reply to your card.) Magnets, too, can be attached to a card front to decorate it and provide a gift for the recipient. A photo, stamped and embossed medallion, or other decorative design can easily be made into a magnet by purchasing a self-adhesive magnetic strip and placing it on the back of the piece you created. Use foam adhesive or place a thin piece of metal on the back of the panel below to hold it in place.

Tea Bag Folded Cards

Tea bag folding, a type of origami originally done using printed packets from tea bags, is a great way to create a medallion to decorate the front of a folded card. Many designs are created by folding eight identical squares of paper in a particular way and then gluing them together to create a pinwheel-like structure.

Sandy Stern, whose cards are pictured, designed the delightful variation of a traditional tea bag structure that appears below. She explains, "In Holland, where tea bag folding started, it is often called 'kaleidoscope' folding," noting that "creating the medallions is like playing with a kaleidoscope. Seemingly insignificant details in a picture can

form the most beautiful patterns." Sandy often creates windows in her folded card stock in which to place the medallions so the back of the structure can also be enjoyed.

A stunning card by Sandy Stern, featuring a tea bag medallion within a cutout window. The marker border is drawn using the corner punch as a guide. Stamp by Inkadinkado. Corner punch by Fiskars.

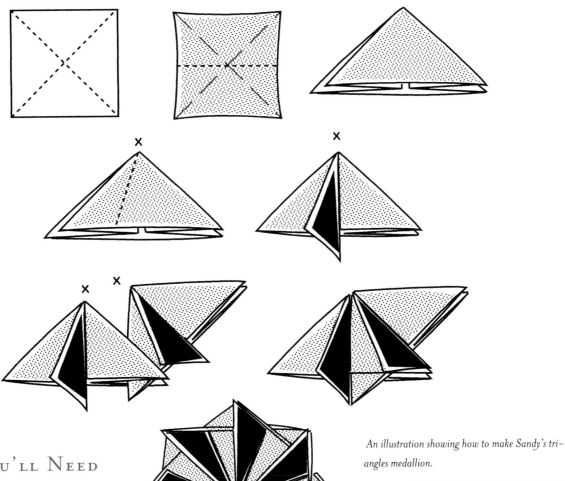

What You'll Need

Paper. Use a paper that is light-weight, yet crisp enough to hold a fold. Commercial tea bag paper already laid out in identical 2" squares is ideal for beginners. A printed paper with an all-over pattern or a pre-cut square origami paper 3" or smaller can also be easily used to make medallions for cards.

Metal-edged ruler and X-acto knife. For cutting out the squares of paper. (A C-Thru metal-edged ruler is preferred.)

Glue. A glue pen is perfect for assembling folded structures. White glue and a toothpick might also be used.

Creating the Triangles Medallion

Start with a square of paper facing you wrong-side-up. Create a valley fold across each diagonal. Turn the paper over so the patterned side is facing you and create a horizontal valley fold, as shown above. Pick up the paper so that the wrong side is facing you and push the center of the square

An illustration showing how to make Sandy's triangles medallion.

slightly until the center pops outward. Then, using your index fingers, push the sides into the center of the square, creating the triangular structure shown.

Position the paper so that the point (X) is up and fold one of the side flaps toward you to the center line of the structure, creating a narrow wing. Create eight of these structures, making sure that every module faces in the same direction when you make the horizontal fold and again when you make the final side-flap wing fold. The kaleidoscopic effect of the medallion will be lost if all parts of the medallion are not identical.

ASSEMBLING THE MEDALLION

To assemble the medallion, apply glue between two of the side flaps of one module and insert a second one between these glued flaps with the points marked X touching.

Make sure that the wing is not placed in the glue. Continue with the rest of the modules until all eight are assembled and the structures form a continuous circle.

CREATING THE CARD

The finished triangles medallion can be glued to the front of a square or rectangular folded card embellished with a stamped, stenciled, or calligraphic greeting. If you create a windowed card like Sandy's your recipient can enjoy the front as well as the back of the medallion. Sandy created her card by sandwiching eight points (north, south, east, and west) of her triangles medallion between two square windows cut in pieces of card stock.

What You'll Need

Cards. You need a folded card and a coordinating flat card cut ⅛" smaller all around than the front of the folded card

Assembled tea bag medallion.

X-acto knife and metal-edged ruler.

Pencil.

Removable tape.

Fine-tipped glue pen or white glue and a toothpick Use the toothpick to apply the glue.

Dry adhesive.

Cutting the window in the flat card. The smaller interior square was made by tracing around the opening in the folded green card.

Rubber stamps, punches, stencils, or other embellishments (optional).

Technique

Sandy used the following steps to create her windowed card.

1. Fold a triangles medallion variation as shown. Since both sides of the medallion will show, choose one that looks interesting on both the front and back.

2. Measure the medallion from the tip of one point to the tip of the opposite point.

3. In the front of the folded green card, cut a square about ½" smaller than the medallion measurement.

4. Use removable tape to hold the tan (flat) card stock in the desired position on the front of the card. Then flip the card over and trace the square window onto the back of the tan card stock. Remove the tape and draw a square that is ⅛" larger *all around* (above). (For example, if the folded green card has a 2¼" window, the flat tan card will have a 2½" window.)

5. On the back of the triangles medallion (the flat side), dot glue on the tips of the pairs of points at top, bottom, left, and right. Do not put glue on the other points; they will not overlap the edges of the window. Attach the medallion to the front of the window in the folded card.

6. Embellish the flat card as desired.

7. Apply double-stick tape or adhesive film to the back of the flat card, including the edge of the window.

8. Attach the flat card over the medallion, keeping the valley-folded flaps on the outside.

Note: You may also try circular or octagonal windows, using a circle cutter or shape templates. For a circle or an octagon you will be able to attach all eight pairs of points to the card.

Making Pop-up Cards

Pop-up cards have the most dimension and are probably the most exciting greetings you can send. No matter how old the recipient is, the delight of having a card explode out in a pop-up surprise will make any adult feel like a kid again. Most pop-up cards look much more complicated than they really are and many people are put off by the thought of all the measuring required to make what some call a "paper-engineered" card. (That name alone is intimidating.)

It's true that if your measurements and folds are off, it will show and your card may not open or close properly. It is also true that if you have to keep fingering a paper to figure out which folds to push in and which to bring forward, that, too, will be evident in the finished card. For this reason, it makes sense to design models of simple pop-up cards on inexpensive graph paper first, so you can determine where to cut and practice folding before you make the finished work on stiffer, more expensive paper or card stock.

To begin exploring pop-ups, buy an inexpensive graph paper tablet laid out with four squares to the inch. With a sheet of graph paper and a pair of scissors or X-acto knife you can create cards with pop-up shelves and exploding cards in minutes—without measuring a thing.

A pop-up card by Sandy Stern, featuring steps that support rubber-stamped, hand-painted, and cutout images. Sandy designed the jester stamps using clip art.

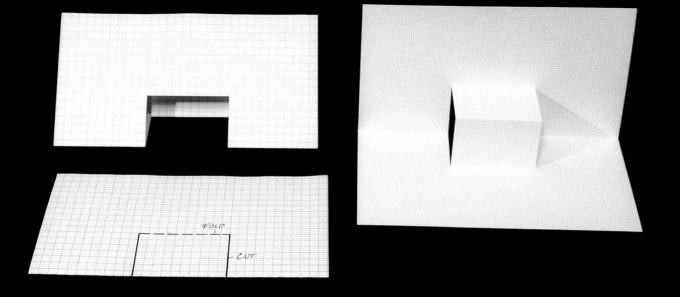

To make a step or pop-up support for a rubber-stamped paper cutout, like that in Sandy's card, fold a sheet of graph paper in half and, near the center of the sheet, make two slits (above). Mine are seven blocks deep and a couple of inches apart. Cut on the lines and be sure to end each cut at the bot-tom of the same square. Your slits will be even and parallel. Fold and crease the flap of paper you just created along the dotted line that connects the base of each slit. Move it backward and then forward to crease it in both directions.

Now open your folded paper enough to push the flap through

Above: A finished single pop-up step or ledge and graph paper practice sheets showing where to cut and fold and how the sheet looks when the flap is pushed through.

to the other side and flatten it. The top of the flap, which was originally a mountain fold, will become a

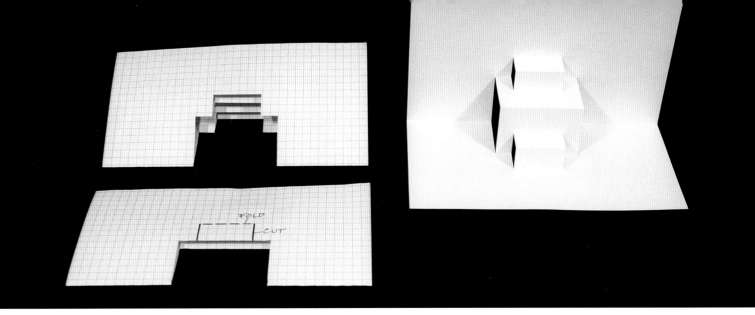

Above: The finished triple pop-up steps and graph paper practice sheets showing where to cut and fold and how the sheet looks when the second set of steps is pushed through.

Opposite: An accordion-folded card by Joan B. Machinchick with pop-up steps that showcase her art. Joan's cards feature beautiful calligraphy, but she always leaves a blank page for writing a personal message.

---

valley fold. Your paper will look like the upper left image (opposite) when the paper is flat. Use a bone folder to sharpen the paper creases. Now open the paper to see a little step, which, when made on heavier paper, can be used as a pop-up support for a picture or photograph. When viewed vertically on an accordion-folded card like the one by Joan Machinchick opposite, the ledges become little windows to showcase the artwork on her card.

To practice making two more steps, cut two more slits, each two blocks in from the first ones. Make these about three blocks deep and follow the same procedure as before to fold the paper in both directions and push the flaps through. Your paper will look like the upper left part of the figure above when it's flat. When opened, it will sport multiple steps or ledges.

Transferring the Design to Heavy Paper

Card stock (the best choice for crisp designs), or a cover stock like Canson Mi Teintes, are good papers to use for your final card. The papers are thin enough to crease with light scoring and sturdy enough to hold the crease. To transfer your graph paper pop-up to heavier paper (without measuring!), just lay the slit design over heavy paper, making sure that the fold lines run cross-grain. Although this seems contrary to the rules, it helps produce pop-ups that hold their shape. Mark the end of each cut with a pin prick, connect the pin marks with a metal ruler, and cut parallel slits. You can repeatedly use your graph paper design in this way, as a pattern.

Note: When working with very heavy paper, you will need to score the base of the flaps before attempting to crease and push them through to the front.

Creating a Backing

To create a backing for a pop-up card that won't bind when you attempt to fold the card, cut a piece of card stock slightly shorter and more narrow than your pop-up. (OK, you might have to measure this.) Cut the paper backing in half and glue each half to the pop-up, letting the fold line extend. Be sure to keep glue off the parts of the structure that are meant to rise, or they won't be able to operate.

Creating a "Farmer's Purse" Exploding Card

Mary Howe sent me this structure, which she often uses to create her amazing music box cards that are activated by a button on the base of the card. The structure is begun almost exactly as the tea bag card shown on page 104. Start with a square of paper facing you, but right-side-up this time (opposite). Create a valley fold across each diagonal. Turn the paper over so the wrong side is facing you and create a horizontal valley fold, as shown. Pick up the paper so that the right side is facing you and push the center of the square slightly until the center pops outward. Then, using your index fingers, push the sides into the center of the square, creating the triangular structure shown. Be aware that you will be looking at the wrong side of the paper or card stock.

Now fold each of the two side flaps forward to the center of the triangle and backward to crease them in both directions. Flip the triangle over and do the same with the side flaps on the back of the structure. Now gently maneuver all folded flaps to form the structure pictured. The inside of the purse will feature the patterned or good side of your paper. To finish the card, create a backing for your folded structure by cutting card stock the same height as the purse square and half the width. Use a dry adhesive to adhere the card together, making sure that the point at the top of the purse (when it is collapsed) lines up with the center of the folded card stock.

PHOTO BY KEN WOISARD.

Above: Mary Howe's "Happy Birthday, Jean" features a picture of her friend's springer spaniel. The "farmer's purse" folded card features a musical button in the dog's mouth that plays the sound of a barking dog.

Opposite: An illustration showing how to create a "farmer's purse" folded card.

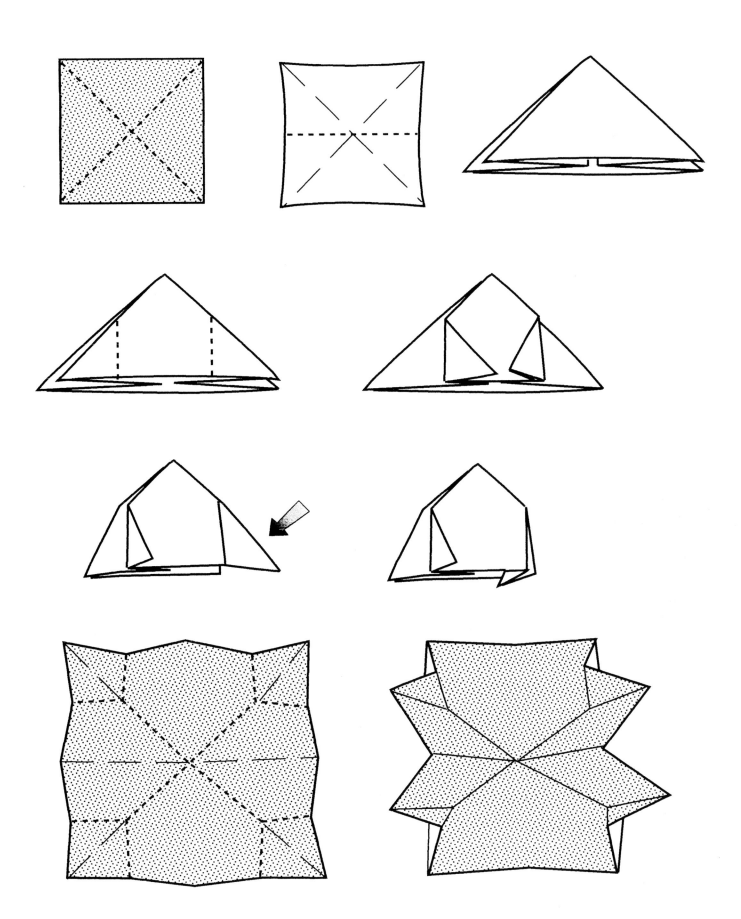

The Double Accordion-folded Pop-up

Pop-out panels that resemble the ledges previously shown are easy to make by creating an accordion-folded card and then cutting slits in the pages to accommodate a second set of accordion-folded pages inserted in them. Joan Machinchick's fine calligraphy helps make this a simple but elegant way to present a pop-up greeting.

Above: Joan B. Machinchick's simple but elegant calligraphic greeting features a second set of accordion-folded pages that pop up when the card is opened.

Below: A view from the top of the card to show how the second set of pages is attached by being passed through slits in the first set of folded pages.

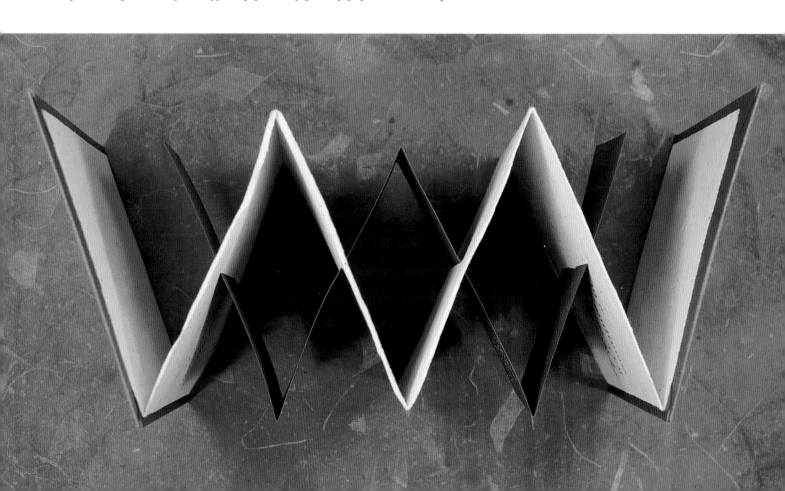

$\mathscr{A}$n Exploding Card Variation

An easy variation of the previous fold that creates an exploding card begins with the patterned or message side of the paper facing you. Using a square of paper (see next page), make two horizontal valley folds—one in each direction. Then flip the paper over and, with the wrong side up, make a diagonal valley fold. Flip the paper to the right side again and push slightly in the middle to finish this simple structure. Adhere it, points up, to a folded or two-part backing.

An "exploding card" invitation created by Joan B. Machinchick.

a birthday bash
Dan's
50th

413 SEVENTH STREET NW

WASHINGTON, DC

RSVP 301-229-7086

NILA

dining
&
dancing

CREATING "STAR CARD" HANGING ORNAMENTS

The variation of the exploding card previously mentioned can be used to create elaborate cards, sometimes called "star cards," that open to become hanging ornaments. To create a star card similar to the one shown by Lynne Carnes (opposite page), make five exploding card variations.

Then, instead of adhering their points to a backing, adhere one point of each structure to an adjoining card.

Lynne has sandwiched pieces of ribbon between the first and last points on the structure and the rigid covers she has made for the card. For a more simple design, holes can be punched in the first and last points and ribbon included with the collapsed structure to be strung through

these holes when the card is opened. The papercutting and calligraphy on Lynne's card might be replaced with stamped or stenciled designs.

Opposite: Lynne Carnes adhered a series of cut-paper "exploding card" structures together to create a card that is also a hanging decoration.

Below: Diagram for the "exploding card."

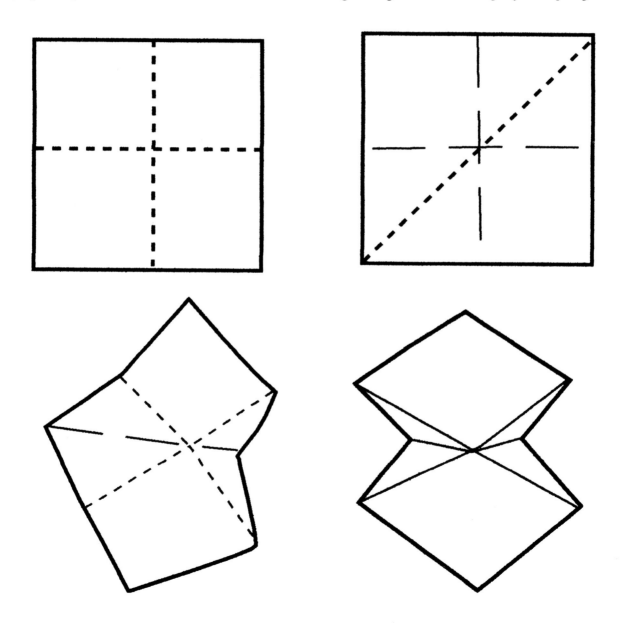

creative card
LETTERING

I f you choose to place words or phrases on the outside of your card, it's fairly easy to find a stamp, stencil, or embossing plate with appropriate lettering to coordinate with it. Sometimes there's a stamp or stencil with a great message for the inside of your card, too, in which case all you have to do in your own handwriting is neatly sign your name. Computer type is another option for cards that are run through your printer or have a computer typewritten message adhered to them. There are times, however, when the words you want to say are so pointed that they don't exist ready-made, or the card you are sending really calls for a personal touch. And, of course, there's the envelope that carries your card. If first impressions count, you don't want to have your recipient's address running downhill or, worse yet, so illegible that the card comes back to you. The answer to these problems—you guessed it—is to improve your handwriting.

An amazing fourteen-layer card by Lea Everse made with a Letra Jet "airbrush" and alcohol pens using a torn paper mask. The ornamental dots that decorate the calligraphy were made with fabric paint.

Tricks and Techniques to Improve Your Handwriting

The best way to acquire beautiful handwriting is to enroll in a calligraphy course and practice diligently. It does require a commitment and a good deal of retraining to undo habits you've spent years repeating. There are several tricks and techniques that can help you improve your handwriting without actually taking a course, however, and some of them are very simple.

CORRECTING POORLY FORMED LETTERS

The easiest way to correct poorly formed letters is to slow down. Writing a personal greeting should not be done with the same speed that you fill out your grocery list. Our lives are so fast paced that it is hard to slow down, but doing so will help your handwriting immensely. Speed-written letters tend to collapse and "e"s wind up looking like "i"s, "t"s like "l"s, etc. Take a look at a note that you've dashed off and see how many letters could easily be mistaken for another if you didn't already know what the words were. Try writing extra large for awhile to retrain

A card made by using rubber stamps in paste with a thermal-embossed rubber-stamped greeting by Grace Taormina.

Calligraphic ornamentation and drawing enhance the lettering on this holiday greeting by Joan B. Machinchick.

yourself to form letters better and remember the sage advice to "dot your 'i's and cross your 't's"!

CORRECTING INCONSISTENT LETTERFORMS OR ATTACHMENTS

Many people, including me, have the nasty habit of creating a single letter many different ways, depending upon which letter it attaches to. We flip-flop our "r"s or the letter "s" and never really decide how we want to form the letter. Look over your writing and decide how you wish to make the letter in question, then force yourself to be consistent . At first you will write more slowly, but soon you will retrain yourself and become comfortable with making consistent letterforms.

STRAIGHTENING LETTERS THAT LEAN FORWARD AND BACK

Do your "i"s and "t"s slant back and forth on the page? Speed writing often makes us slant our letters erratically, but being unable to control your pen because of an uneven writing surface or because you are extremely tense may also be part of the problem. Slowing down, working on a padded surface instead of a dented tabletop, and loosening up by making playful doodles with your pen will help. Try playing music, as well, to relax you.

PREVENTING WRITING FROM GOING UP- OR DOWN-HILL

This is a common lefty's problem because of the way the pen is held, not a sign of a depressed or overly exuberant personality. Poor pos-

ture or writing on a page cocked at a strange angle because of a cluttered desk can also contribute to the problem. Create a better writing area and write on a slanted surface to help control your posture. Slip a ruled sheet behind thin white cards or place a sheet of paper on top of the card you're lettering, using its top edge as a guide until you get the first line straight. You can also rule a single erasable line at the top of your page and concentrate on writing each line parallel to the line above. Some people use a fork to make nearly invisible parallel lines on envelopes so that they can neatly address them.

FINDING THE CORRECT WRITING TOOL

Another way to help your penmanship is to find a writing implement that fits your hand and style of writing. I always write most neatly with a pencil or wide-nibbed pen. Fine-tipped pens don't work for me at all. Some pens drag when I use them or waver as I letter with them. These same pens are favorites of my husband. Calligraphers, too, have their pen preferences. Lettering artists Jill Quillian and Carole Maurer recommend the ZIG "Memory System," a group of pens with various sized and shaped tips available in many colors including white, silver, and gold. Lea Everse prefers Staedtler Pigment Liners with a chisel-tip calligraphy nib (opposite). Paul Maurer (no relation to Carole) prefers to work with Coit or Speedball chisel-edged pens.

The best way to find a good writing tool is to go to a shop that sells writing implements and try several pens to see how they affect your writing. The weight and balance of the pen and the ease with

Above: Nancy Culmone touched parts of her gouache lettering with white to produce these variegated letters.

Opposite: Lea Everse had one of her large calligraphic works reduced to reproduce on her cards. Notice how the way she has composed the spiral lettering continues the perspective shown on the drawing in the center of the card. The poem, "Macavity the Mystery Cat," is by T. S. Eliot.

which the ink flows from it will work with or against you depending upon your writing idiosyncrasies. (If you use a pen with a cap, be sure to place the cap on the end of it when writing—it is important to the balance of the pen.) Consider how you want to use the pen as well. Do you want something with a narrow nib for addressing envelopes, or a wide-nibbed pen with a chisel tip for writing a greeting that will be more in scale with the front of your card?

Macavity's a Mystery Cat: he's called the Hidden Paw—for he's the master criminal who can defy the law. He's the bafflement of Scotland Yard, the Flying Squad's despair: for when they reach the scene of crime—Macavity's not there! Macavity, Macavity, there's no one like Macavity, he's broken every human law, he breaks the law of gravity. His powers of levitation would make a fakir stare, and when you reach the scene of crime—Macavity's not there! You may seek him in the basement, you may look up in the air—but I tell you once and once again, Macavity's not there! Macavity's a ginger cat, he's very tall and thin; you would know him if you saw him, for his eyes are sunken in. His brow is deeply lined with thought, his head is highly domed; his coat is dusty from neglect, his whiskers are uncombed. He sways his head from side to side, with movements like a snake; and when you think he's half asleep, he's always wide awake. Macavity, Macavity, there's no one like Macavity, for he's a fiend in feline shape, a monster of depravity. You may meet him in a by-street, you may see him in the square, but when a crime's discovered, then Macavity's not there! He's outwardly respectable. They say he cheats at cards. And his footprints are not found in any file of Scotland Yard's. And when the larder's looted, or the jewel-case is rifled, or when the milk is missing, or another Peke's been stifled, or the greenhouse glass is broken, and the trellis past repair—Ay, there's the wonder of the thing! Macavity's not there! And when the Foreign Office find a treaty's gone astray, or the Admiralty lose some plans and drawings by the way, there may be a scrap of paper in the hall or on the stair, but it's useless to investigate—Macavity's not there! And when the loss has been disclosed, the Secret Service say: 'It must have been Macavity!'—but he's a mile away. You'll be sure to find him resting, or a-licking of his thumbs, or engaged in doing complicated long division sums. Macavity, Macavity, there's no one like Macavity, there never was a cat of such deceitfulness and suavity. He always has an alibi, and one or two to spare: at whatever time the deed took place, Macavity wasn't there! And they say that all the cats whose wicked deeds are widely known—I might mention Mungojerrie, I might mention Griddlebone—are nothing more than agents for the cat who all the time just controls their operations: the Napoleon of Crime!

*L*earning Simple *I*talic Handwriting

Using whatever type of implement you prefer, it's easiest to begin improving your handwriting by learning the italic hand. Although a calligraphy course would be most helpful, the tips and techniques offered below will help you make some positive changes in your handwriting and write greetings and address cards more neatly, without sacrificing the personality of your own hand-writing.

The italic lettering examples and suggestions that follow are from calligrapher Jill Quillian. Jill maintains that our handwriting often falls apart because, "In kindergarten we are taught the ball and stick method of writing. Then in second grade we switch to a slanted cursive with loops and joins. Most of us do not stick with this long enough to master it. By middle school we are doing a mix-ture of printing and cursive and our

writing often becomes illegible."

Jill explains that because the letters in the italic hand are made with only one or two strokes and because the ascender letters like "l" and descender letters like "p" have no loops, they are less likely to become illegible. She explains that the basic italic alphabet is based on an elliptical "O" and

---

Italic capital letters with and without serifs.

ABCDEFGHIJKLMNOP
QRSTUVWXYYZZ

ABCDEFGHIJKLMNOP
QRSTUVWXYZ

ascender line
waist line
base line or writing line
descender line

otg abp egt

Above: The italic letters on the ruled lines show how far the ascending letters should rise above the "waist" line and how far the descending ones should extend below the writing line. Example by Jill A. Quillian.

Right: Italic handwriting examples by Jill Quillian showing alphabets and letter families with and without serifs.

---

that all letters are slanted 5 to 10 degrees to the right.

Jill advocates learning the basic skeletal italic letter forms first and later adding serifs—entry and exit strokes—which allow us to write faster (opposite). She cautions that these joins should not become ornate additions to letter shapes, but just simple connections to other letters.

The italic letters on the ruled lines above show how far ascending letters (b, d, h, k, l, and f) rise above the waist line and descending ones (g, j, p, q, and y) extend below the writing line.

The following letters are made in one stroke: a, b, c, g, h, k, l, m, n, o, q, r, s, u, v, w, y, and z. Two-stroke letters include d, e, f, i, j, p, t, and x. Jill suggests grouping similarly made letters

Simple Italic Handwriting
Letter families with and without serifs,
5° to 10° slant.

adgq	adgq
oecs	oecs
nmrhbkp	nmrhbkp
ftz	ftz
xs	xs
jp	jp
il	il
uy	uy
vw	vw

Practice first with no serifs. Build a strong foundation. abcdefghijklmnopqrstuvwxyz
Later add entrance and exit strokes (serifs) which will make natural joins.
abcdefghijklmnopqrstuvwxyz

together and practicing writing them as letter families, as shown above.

If you carry your italic examples with you and practice tracing

or writing them while waiting for appointments or when stuck in freeway traffic, you'll soon see a difference in your handwriting and lettering skills.

*U*sing Broad-edged Pens

Calligraphic lettering that features beautiful thick and thin lines is the result of using a pen that has a broad edge. Broad-edged pen italic calligraphy can be written with square-edged nibs, fountain pens, or chisel-edged markers. The italic hand can still be followed but the pen must be held at a constant 45-degree angle. If you try to manipulate the pen, you won't be able to write with the entire edge of the nib, and the thick-and-thin effect will be lost.

Experiment with chisel-edged calligraphy markers by drawing long thin vertical strokes with the side of the pen and then drawing the pen across the paper in a series of hill-and-valley strokes as shown by Jill Quillian (opposite). Write slowly and let the pen follow your arm movements. Try some flourishes for the fun of it and spend some time getting to know this new writing instrument. Address a few envelopes using thick and thin strokes to make

decorative lines as a guide for the address or to make a decorative border design for a card or envelope.

Below: A broad-edged pen uncial alphabet by Paul Maurer. Calligraphy books can offer you many lettering styles to trace and practice.

Opposite: Examples by Jill A. Quillian showing how to familiarize yourself with a chisel-edged pen by making hill and valley strokes.

To get the feel of a chisel-edged tool, hold the tip at 45° continuously and make mountains, valleys and hills. These can become borders, too.

Decorative Lettering Styles

You can add personality to your written greetings by decorating your letters with outlines, shadows, and dots as well as by writing on a curve or letting the letters bounce up and down. In addition to making your card lettering unique, these techniques hide some lettering imperfections. You can trace or draw your letters and your decorative accents lightly with a #2 pencil and then go over them in colored pen or markers if necessary until you gain confidence, but often just practicing these techniques on scrap paper a number of times will help you get a feel for them.

Calligrapher Carole Maurer contributed instructions on successful letter tracing for book pages in *Art of the Scrapbook* (Watson-Guptill Publications, New York). Her technique will work for tracing letters for card designs as well.

1. Draw a pencil line for the base of the letters or words you wish to copy on a piece of tracing paper. Place the tracing paper over the letters to be transferred and carefully trace them with a sharp pencil.

2. Turn the paper over and scribble with a soft pencil on the back of your traced lettering. Dab up the excess pencil carbon with a tissue to prevent smearing. Turn the paper over so that the clean side is facing you.

3. Use a C-Thru ruler to draw a light pencil baseline on the card where you want the letters to appear. Position the tracing paper on the line you have just drawn—centering the lettering or offsetting it, as you choose. Use removable tape to position the tracing paper in place. Use a sharp pencil and trace over the letters again. The letters will be transferred to your paper in light pencil marks. Go over the letters with a marker or pen, making adjustments to the letters as necessary.

By making dots, zigzags, and scallops and adding diluted wet ink to a still-wet stroke, you can create decorative initials for the front of a card. Examples by Paul Maurer.

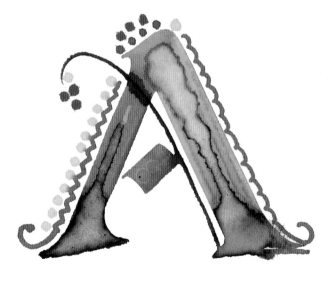

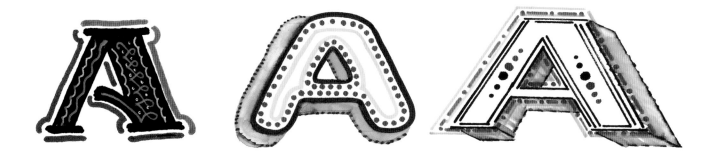

When making letters to be outlined, it's a good idea to leave a little more space around each letter than normal. Try to maintain a constant distance between your letters and their outlines. Drop shadows can be made to the left or right of the letter and may butt against it or be made a short distance from it in a single line or in a shadow line with additional ornamentation. Staggered letters that bounce up and down will be easiest to make if you pencil light horizontal lines on your card or envelope to create different guide lines on which to place alternate letters. You can let your letters tumble back and forth at different angles as you draw them. Letters can also increase or decrease in size as they form a word or phrase to add more emphasis.

Many calligraphers use a compass, a grid atop a light box, a rotating disc, or a tool like the

Above: Drop shadows with or without ornamentation can be made to the left or right of a letter or outline it all around, as shown in this work by Paul Maurer.

Below: The horizontal lines on these letters that bounce up and down help determine letter placement. The diagonal lines help keep the angle of slanted letters uniform. If pencil lines are drawn lightly they can be erased when the lettering is done. Lettering by Paul Maurer.

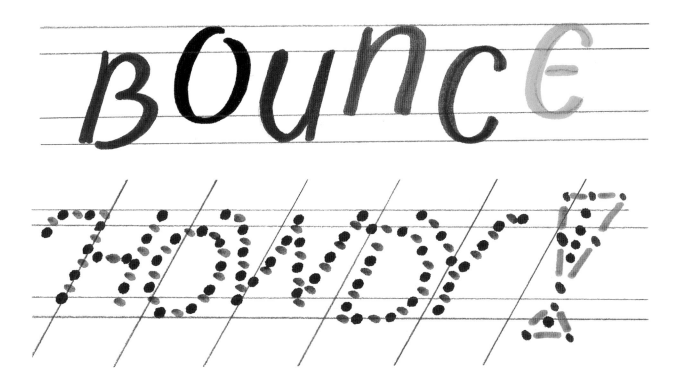

flexible curve or plastic French curve template.

Another way to create waved lettering, also recommended by Carole Maurer, is to draw a gentle wave with a pencil in the center of a piece of card stock. Use scissors or an X-acto knife and cut along the wavy line. Mark the two pieces of card stock "top" and "bottom" so you don't accidentally reverse them. With removable tape, adhere the bottom piece to the card you want to write on. Draw a light pencil line, following the wave. Remove and place the corresponding piece above the line you've just drawn at the desired height of your letters and draw the top line. After creating the waved lettering on your card, erase the pencil lines.

circle/ruler template by EK Success to draw different circle sizes and create parallel lines in which to pen a curved greeting. Lea Everse has devised a more simple method that works well. She creates parallel lines by drawing with two pencils bound together with a rubber band. Lea sometimes binds an eraser between them to create more distance. Then she'll trace around a plate or jar lid to easily create a set of curved lines to letter between. After the lettering is done she can erase the lines.

Parallel gentle waves in which to draw your letters can be made in a similar fashion by using the bound pencils to follow waved patterns created with a draftman's

Above left: Calligraphy written in a circle is featured on this multilayered card by Lea Everse.

Below: Writing "on a wave" is featured in this card by Lea. Stamped image unknown.

Multicolored and Eccentric Lettering

Multicolored lettering can help create a sumptuous card or invitation like that shown by Joan Machinchick (below). If working with chisel-edged markers, you can create a letter in a light blue, for instance, and letter over it partway with violet or other colored markers. Many calligraphers and card artists work with opaque gouache paints, which can be used in a similar way. Blended letters can be made by writing in one color (orange, for instance) and touching the top of the wet letter with another color like red. Touching the center or several areas of the letter with a pen holding white or colored gouache will also produce attractive multicolored letters.

Paul Maurer prefers to take a more serendipitous approach. He often loads his pen with Higgins or Luma ink by dipping part of it into two different colors of ink and sometimes uses a brush to apply a third color to his pen.

A sumptuous diagonal-folded birthday invitation with multicolored lettering by Joan B. Machinchick.

abcdefghijklmnopq
rstuvwxyz & etc.

As he writes, the inks blend together and produce beautiful hues that fade in and out. He readily admits that this technique isn't highly controllable and that sometimes you "hope for the best" and quickly add another color ink if things "start to go bad."

Ornamentation in the form of dots, dashes, and wavy colored lines added to a single letter or used to create the letter can make a wonderful decorative design for the front of a card. The examples provided by Paul Maurer (opposite) show how you can create colorful

Paul Maurer produced multicolored lettering with beautiful hues that fade in and out by loading his pen with different colors of Higgins and Luma inks.

and playful words or initials with gel pens and markers. Lightly pencil-ruled lines showing where

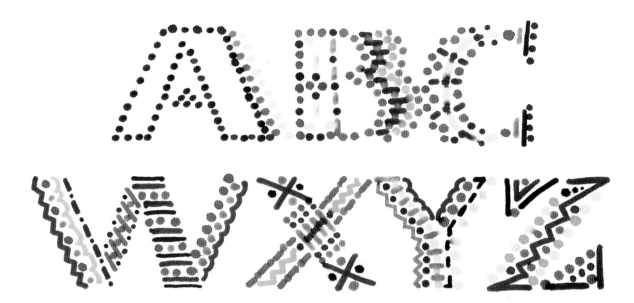

the tops and bottoms of the letters should begin and end will help keep your letters a uniform height. Lightly penciled parallel slanted lines will keep the angle of your slanted letters more consistent. Paul suggests carefully tracing or drawing a pencil outline for each of the letters to keep them a uniform size.

Books on calligraphic ornamentation can give you ideas to trace or alter. When you've gained

some experience handling a broad-edged pen, you might try some letter ornamentation by combining marker and broad-edged pen work and touching wet ink with a bit of water to let it pool into a very fluid diffused design. Ornate initials or names on the front of a card will often wind up framed on your recipient's wall.

Special pens can be used to make your lettering or letter ornamentation stand out. There

Above: Paul used gel pens and markers to create these playful letters, which are composed of dots, dashes, and wavy lines. He advocates studying cartoon lettering to get fresh ideas for card art.

Below: Ornate initials and names are always welcome art on the front of a card. Paul often uses a multiple-line pen that contains a segmented nib to do decorative lettering. By touching parts of the letter with water or another color ink while the first ink applied is still wet, you can create very fluid blended letters.

Left: Jill A. Quillian's delightful card features a letter decorated with colored pencil and calligraphic ornamentation around the central paste-paper panel.

Below: Eccentric lettering on this First Day Cover by Cathy Rogge reflects the lines of the sail featured on the stamp and the photocopy of the stamp that decorates the envelope.

can press different metallic foils into. Zig embossing markers have a slow-drying ink that lets you pen a greeting and then emboss it with colored embossing powders. Finally, Zebra Super-Marble Gel Pens are another new tool that contain several gel colors in one pen. They deposit beautiful shifting colors as you write.

Eccentric lettering that reflects the theme or design of a card or envelope can also be exciting. The lettering on the envelope by Cathy Rogge (below) perfectly

are several to choose from. Krylon Leafing Markers leave a shimmering line of color that resembles foil when you write with them. Leafing Adhesive Pens allow you to write with an adhesive that you

Above: Jill Quillian used elongated eccentric lettering on her paste-paper–decorated card celebrating America.

Right: Jill's eccentric lettering follows the wave design on her paste-paper–decorated envelope.

mimics the waves and curve of the sail on the stamp and photocopied enlargement on her envelope. The elongated lettering on the card and the increasing and decreasing size letters on the envelope by Jill Quillian (above and right) are other examples of how eccentric lettering can be done.

Stamping, Stenciling, and Using Computer-generated Letters

As mentioned previously, you'll have no trouble finding stencils and rubber stamps that can convey your greetings. There are even illuminated alphabet stamps that can be used with embossing powders or foils to produce an elegant card design. Individual letter stamps can be used to make a casual greeting by cutting stamped and colored letters out and sprinkling them across the card front to spell a word.

Brass embossing plates that spell words and phrases can be used to

emboss and/or stencil a message for your greeting either directly on your card or on a separate paper that is then cut and adhered to the front of your card like a book plate. The "word plate" can be layered with other papers and affixed with foam tape to create a dimensional addition to your greeting.

Computer lettering is another option to use for your cards—but only while you are perfecting your hand-lettering skills! Actually, for multiples of cards and invitations this may be a good idea, but these cards will certainly lack the "soul" of the handprinted ones. There are many typefaces that you can print out and trace from or print directly on your card. Even basic word processing programs give you interesting variations of font size, letter spacing, and color for creating lettering on your cards.

If you have professional graphic programs like Adobe Photoshop or Macromedia Freehand you can fill a letterform with patterns, color gradients, or even photographic elements. Type can be placed on a curving line or within a shape like a pine tree or a heart. If you are not computer literate, photocopy shops can usually offer you several styles of lettering and feed information directly to a photocopy machine that will print text on various kinds of paper or directly on your cards.

Opposite: Sandy Stern mounted stamped and embossed phrases on paper tiles to give a festive feeling to her pop-up jester card (interior shown on page 107). Dance bells and metallic ribbons continue the theme. Stamps by Printworks.

Below: Fred B. Mullett's leaf-printed envelope was run through a printer to receive computer-generated lettering.

FRED B. MULLETT
Stamps from Nature Prints
P.O. Box 94502 USA
Seattle, WA 98124
person – 206.624.5723 fax – 206.903.8202

Diane Maurer
PO Box 78
Spring Mills, PA
16875

Final Thoughts

Although it will take you years to approach the skill level of some of the calligraphers and card designers whose work is shown, your lettering, design, and paper art skills will improve with each new card you make. Your greetings and invitations will surprise, touch, and flatter friends, who will realize how much they mean to you. Although you will have an enjoyable and relaxing time creating handcrafted cards, the greatest reward will come from seeing the delight of the people who receive them.

Opposite: Detail of a card by Beth Aten and Paula Swett in which printed, stamped, dyed, painted, and collaged papers were joined with a sewing machine. The stitching is an integral part of the composition.

Below: Nancy L. Cook lettered the word "peace," then cut it out and accordion-folded it to create this pop-up lettered greeting.

Further Reading

Charatan, Karen. *ABC ZIG Calligraphy.* New Jersey: EK Success, 1993.

Dawson, Sophie. *The Art and Craft of Papermaking.* Philadelphia: Running Press, 1992.

Dubay, Inga and Barbara Getty. *Italic Letters: Calligraphy & Handwriting.* Portland, Oregon: Portland State University Continuing Education Press, 1992.

Hiebert, Helen. *The Papermaker's Companion.* Pownal, VT: Storey Books, 2000.

Maurer-Mathison, Diane. *The Art of Making Paste Papers.* New York: Watson-Guptill Publications, 2002.

Maurer-Mathison, Diane. *The Handcrafted Letter.* Pownal, VT: Storey Books, 2001.

Maurer-Mathison, Diane. *Art of the Scrapbook.* New York: Watson-Guptill Publications, 2000.

Maurer-Mathison, Diane. *The Ultimate Marbling Handbook.* New York: Watson-Guptill Publications, 1999.

Maurer-Mathison, Diane with Jennifer Philippoff. *Paper Art.* New York: Watson-Guptill Publications, 1997.

Noble, Mary and Adrian Waddington. *The Art of Color Calligraphy.* Philadelphia: Running Press, 1997.

Weinberg, Suze. *The Art of Rubber Stamping.* New York: Sterling Publishing Co. Inc., 2000.

Pat Blevins created the dramatic diagonal embossing on this card by repeatedly drawing a stylus along the straight edge of an Art Deckle ruler placed beneath her folded card.

Contributors

Beth Aten and Paula Swett
Lewsisburg, PA
www.magpienet.biz

Elaine Benedict
Lake Forest, IL
benedict@attbi.com

Pat Blevins
Englewood, FL
www.artdeckle.com

Ellen Bruck, ECB Studio
Fallston, MD
410-877-0787

Kimberly Byerly
Delaware, OH
kbyerly1@columbus.rr.com

Lynne Carnes
Tucson, AZ
lynnecarnes@aol.com

Rona Chumbook
Green Valley, AZ
rchumbook@worldnet.att.net

Nancy L. Cook, Paper Designs
Trappe, MD
scheren@chesapeake.net

Nancy Culmone
Serafina, NM
505-421-0077

Leslie Ebert
Portland, OR
www.leslieebert.com

Lea Everse
Lubbock, TX
thelazystamper@aol.com

A rubber-stamped batik card by Vonda Jones.

Barbara Fletcher, Paper*Dimensions*
Billerica, MA
www.paperdimensions.com

Lynell Harlow, Dreamweaver
Stencils
Colton, CA
www.dreamweaverstencils.com

Patti Quinn Hill
Weaverville, NC
pattiquinnhill@mindspring.com

Sandy Hogan
Tucson, AZ
shogan@worldnet.att.net

Mary Howe
Stonington, ME
mch@media2.hypernet.com

Roxann Hutchison
Chagrin Falls, OH

Michael Jacobs,
The Creative Zone
Seattle,WA
www.thecreativezone.com

Vonda Jones
Tucson, AZ
danenoodle@aol.com

Jane Koot
State College, PA
814-238-1326

Paula Beardell Krieg
Salem, NY
paulabear4K@yahoo.com

Mary Anne Landfield
Langhorne, PA
quillingtimes@aol.com

Claudia Lee, Claudia Lee Studio
Liberty, TN
paperlee@dtccom.net

Joan B. Machinchick,
Lake Claire Design Studio
Arnold, MD
lakeclaire@toad.net

Paul Maurer
Serafina, NM

Hélène Métivier,
Magenta Rubber Stamps
Sainte-Julie, QC Canada
www.magentastyle.com

Fred B. Mullett
Seattle, WA
www.fredbmullett.com

Jennifer Philippoff
Aaronsburg, PA
j.philippoff@earthlink.net

Jill Quillian, Jill's Quills
Fond du Lac, WI
www.jillsquills.com

Bren Reisinger
Scottsdale, AZ
designs@brensan.com

Kathy Rogge
Green Valley, AZ
lrogge@attglobal.net

Shirley Seigenthaler
State College, PA

Susan Joy Share
Anchorage, AK
907-279-0109

Martha Sparks
Portland, OR
marthasparks@uswest.net

Sandy Stern
Brinklow, MD
postern@erols.com

Grace Taormina, Rubber
Stampede
Oakland, CA
www.deltacrafts.com/rubberstampede

Debra Tlach, Ranger Industries
Tinton Falls, NJ
www.rangerink.com

Betsy Veness
E. Aurora, NY

Brenda Volpe
Hilliard, OH
volpe.1@osu.edu

Suze Weinberg
Freehold, NJ
www.schmoozewithsuze.com

Suppliers

Listed below are manufacturers and mail order suppliers for some of the materials used in this book. The manufacturers sell their products exclusively to art supply and crafts retailers, which are a consumer's most dependable source for card-crafting supplies. Your local retailer can advise you

on purchases and can order a product for you if they don't have it in stock. If you can't find a store in your area that carries a particular item or will accept a request for an order, or if you need special assistance, a manufacturer can direct you to the retailer nearest you that carries their products and will try to answer any technical questions you might have. When purchasing hard-to-find or specialized materials, it's best to deal with specialized mail order and Internet sources.

Diane Maurer Hand Marbled Papers
P.O. Box 78
Spring Mills, PA 16875
814-422-8651
www.dianemaurer.com
Marbling, paste paper, decorative papers, and Boku Undo dye supplies

Dieu Donné Papermill, Inc.
433 Broome Street
New York, NY 10013-2622
212-226-0573
Papermaking supplies, paper

A pop-up card and envelope made from recycled posters by Michael Jacobs. The smaller tab of paper on the extreme right of the card lifts the other sections when it is pulled.

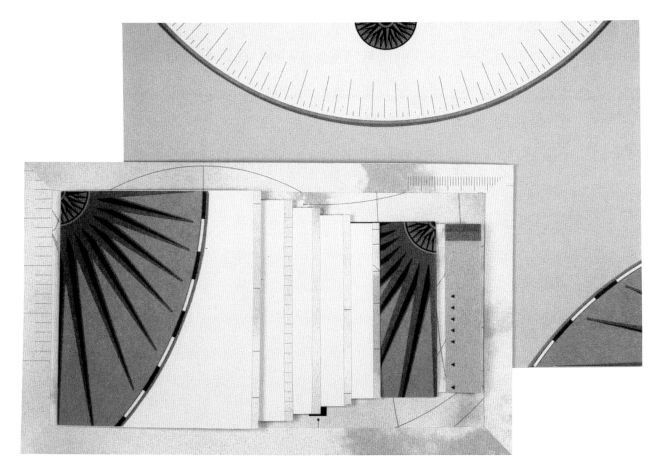

Dreamweaver Stencils
1335 Cindee Lane
Colton, CA 92324
909-824-8343
www.dreamweaverstencils.com
Embossing and stenciling supplies

Factory Express
1720 Coulter
Rio Rancho, NM 87124
800-399-2564
www.factory-express.com
Kuttrimmer paper cutter

Hollanders
407 North Fifth Avenue
Ann Arbor, MI 48104
734-741-7531
www.hollanders.com
Decorative papers

La Papeterie St. Armand
950 Rue Ottawa
Montreal, Quebec
Canada H3C 1S4
514-874-4089
Papermaking supplies, paper

Greg Markim, Inc.
P.O. Box 13245
Milwaukee, WI 53213
800-453-1485
www.arnoldgrummer.com
Papermaking supplies

Magenta Rubber Stamps
2275 Bombardier
Sainte-Julie, Quebéc
Canada, J3E 2J9
www.magentarubberstamps.com
Art stamps inspired by old pictures and prints

Fred B. Mullett
P.O. Box 94502
Seattle, WA 98124
206-624-5723
www.fredbmullett.com
Stamps from nature prints

Nature's Pressed
P.O. Box 212
Orem, UT 84049-0212
800-850-2499
www.naturespressed.com
Pressed leaves and flowers

John Neal, Bookseller
1833 Spring Garden Street
Greensboro, NC 27403
800-369-9598
www.johnnealbooks.com
Books, calligraphy supplies

Paper & Ink Books
15309A Sixes Bridge Road
Emmitsburg, MD 21727
800-736-7772
www.paperinkbooks.com
Books, calligraphy supplies

Paper-Ya & Kakali Handmade
Papers, Inc.
9-1666 Johnston Street
Granville Island
Vancouver, BC
Canada V6H 3S2
604-684-2531
Paper

Ranger Industries
15 Park Road
Tinton Falls, NJ 07724
732-389-3535
www.rangerink.com
Stamping and art supplies

US Art Quest, Inc.
P.O. Box 88
Chelsea, MI 48118
800-200-7848
www.usartquest.com
Stamping and art supplies

Suze Weinberg
11 Bannard Street
Freehold, NJ 07728
732-761-2400
www.schmoozewith suze.com
Stamping and art supplies

Xyron, Inc.
15820 North 84th Street
Scottsdale, AZ 85260
800-793-3523
www.xyron.com
Adhesive and laminating machines

Index

About the Author

DIANE MAURER-MATHISON is recognized internationally as an expert paper artist. Her work is represented in numerous museum collections, including those of the Cooper-Hewitt Museum (New York), the Nelson-Atkins Museum (Kansas City), the Dutch Royal Library (The Netherlands), Harvard University Library (Cambridge), The Süleymaniye Library (Istanbul, Turkey), and The Museum of Antiquities (Urumchi, China). Diane has taught marbling and paste paper design throughout the United States and has made guest appearances on *The Carol Duvall Show, Home Matters,* and *Martha Stewart Living.* She is the author of ten books, including *Paper Art* (Watson-Guptill, 1997), *The Ultimate Marbling Handbook* (Watson-Guptill, 1999), *Art of the Scrapbook: A Guide to Handbinding and Decorating Memory Books, Albums, and Art Journals* (Watson-Guptill, 2000), *The Handcrafted Letter* (Storey Books, 2001), and *The Art of Making Paste Papers* (Watson-Guptill, 2002). Diane lives in Spring Mills, Pennsylvania. Visit her website at www.dianemaurer.com